Linux Comp

LINUX COMPANION
The Essential Guide for Users and System Administrators

Mark F. Komarinski

For book and bookstore information

http://www.prenhall.com

Prentice Hall PTR
Upper Saddle River, New Jersey 07458

Library of Congress Cataloging-in-Publication Data

Komarinski, Mark (Mark F.)
    Linux companion : the essential guide for users and system
    administrators / Mark Komarinski.
        p.   cm.
    Includes index.
    ISBN 0–13–231838–5
    1. Linux.   2. Operating systems (Computers)   I. Title.
QA76.76.063K648   1996
005.4'469—dc20   96–3083
                                                         CIP

Acquisitions editor: Mark L. Taub
Cover designer: DeFranco Design
Cover design director: Jerry Votta
Manufacturing manager: Alexis R. Heydt
Compositor/Production services: Pine Tree Composition, Inc.

© 1996 by Prentice Hall PTR
Prentice-Hall, Inc.
A Simon & Schuster Company
Upper Saddle River, New Jersey 07458

The publisher offers discounts on this book when ordered in
bulk quantities. For more information contact:

> Corporate Sales Department
> Prentice Hall PTR
> One Lake Street
> Upper Saddle River, New Jersey 07458
>
> Phone: 800-382-3419
> Fax: 201-236-7141
> email: corpsales@prenhall.com

Printed in the United States of America
10   9   8   7   6   5   4   3   2   1

ISBN: 0-13-231838-5

Prentice-Hall International (UK) Limited, *London*
Prentice-Hall of Australia Pty. Limited, *Sydney*
Prentice-Hall Canada Inc., *Toronto*
Prentice-Hall Hispanoamericana, S.A., *Mexico*
Prentice-Hall of India Private Limited, *New Delhi*
Prentice-Hall of Japan, Inc., *Tokyo*
Simon & Schuster Asia Pte. Ltd., *Singapore*
Editora Prentice-Hall do Brasil, Ltda., *Rio de Janeiro*

Contents

Acknowledgments

Thanks go out to a lot of people, since a lot of work went into this project.

My thanks to: The Technical Communication Department at Clarkson University, who got me into technical writing in the first place; The Linux Journal, for giving a guy a chance at writing a monthly column; and Mr. Mark Taub at Prentice Hall, for giving a guy a chance at writing an entire book.

To the people who gave functional or emotional support: My family, Amy Rich ("There is no "X-Windows"!"); Lioness Ayres ("You're writing a REAL book?"); Brenda (Hering) Komarinski, who kept me in the real world by getting married to me; Nelson Chadderdon, any quote about him would make him look bad; Chris Haase and his red pen of doom; Dan Corley, who doesn't know a lot about Linux, but can make some darn good ray-traced images; and a lot of other people (you know who you are).

Also thanks to Wizvax Communications for wizvax.net references; the excerpt of the Commercial-HOWTO appears courtesy of Harald Milz (hm@seneca.han.de); MS-DOS and Microsoft are registered trademarks and Windows, Windows 95, and NT are trademarks of Microsoft Corporation, and OS/2 is a trademark of IBM. Other products mentioned are the trademarks of their respective owners.

Mark F. Komarinski

Introduction

Who Should Buy This Book

Do you know DOS? Do you know Windows? Are you sick of using them? Do you want something more than you can find in a shrinkwrapped package? This book is for you. Buy it, use it, and feel good about it.

Who Should Not Buy This Book

If you're new to computers this book is not for you. If you don't know where the power switch is, or how DOS or Windows works, you may be interested in a book more oriented toward a new user.

Note:

You may notice that not all subjects are handled in as much depth as you may like. The reason for this is twofold. First, hardware and software setups change with each installation. My system is undoubtedly different than yours. Another reason is that Linux itself changes. Linux is different from most other software of this magnitude in that there is no central organization that controls the whole operating system. The entire operating system is changing. You have your choice of using many different programs.

If I document a static setup, then the book will be of no use in six months when the kernel has different properties. What I can do (and the purpose of this book) is to show you how Linux works. I'll give you pointers to locations to find specific information. One useful resource is the HOWTO guides. These guides give information about a variety of topics, from connecting to the Internet, to getting your printer to work with your particular system, to discussing Ethernet in great detail. These HOWTO guides are usually included in CD-ROM installations. For those of you with Internet connections, the HOWTO guides are available by FTP and the World Wide Web. See Appendix A for Internet resources.

Linux Companion

CHAPTER 1

- Linux History

- Why Use Linux?

- Where to Get Linux

- Linux Concepts versus DOS Concepts

What Is Linux?

Welcome to the wonderful world of Linux! Just what is Linux? It's an operating system, much like DOS, OS/2, and Windows NT or Windows 95. The operating system is the single most important piece of software on your computer. It allows your hardware and software to work together. Without your operating system, your programs would not be able to find or access all the hardware you have. The big difference between Linux, OS/2, DOS, or Windows NT is that Linux is free.

What does free mean? Free, in this context, doesn't mean that there is no monetary cost involved (there may or may not be). Free means that you are able to take the original source code used in Linux and modify it. You are free to get the source code of just about any other program that the operating system runs. You are free to take one CD and install Linux on as many machines as you want. You are free to have as many users logged in as the hardware can handle. You do not have to buy extra user licenses or anything else. Try it out—it's all there.

Linux History

Linux is an offshoot of a broader type of operating system known as UNIX, which was started in 1969 by a group of researchers at Bell Labs in New Jersey. This group was working on an operating system called Multics. When the project was canceled, this group went ahead and completed the development of the system, calling it UNIX as a play on the original name. Around the same time, the C programming language was developed. Large portions of UNIX were written in C, an easily portable language.

A portable language is one that can be used on multiple platforms. C and Pascal are both examples of portable languages. A C program can be compiled with few changes between an 80386-based machine and a 68040 based machine, such as the Apple Macintosh. Having the operating system written in C allowed the early UNIX developers to compile it on different hardware platforms in a shorter period of time. Before this, most operating systems were written in assembly language, which is specific to each type of computer hardware.

UNIX soon began cropping up in all sorts of locations. One location was the University of California at Berkley. In the late 1970s Berkley took what Bell Labs had, rewrote some of it, and added extensive modifications. The resulting product was known as BSD for Berkley Standard Distribution. The BSD implementation of UNIX included networking support, editors like vi, and changes in the way some programs worked.

Bell Labs could not sell their version (AT&T) of UNIX because of an antitrust agreement, but a few locations were getting licenses from AT&T. In the early 1980s when Bell Labs was broken up, the restriction covering licensing of UNIX was also lifted, and AT&T began selling their version. The BSD and AT&T (also known as SYSV) styles UNIX were installed on machines from IBM, Sun, and DEC, among others.

The name UNIX was owned by AT&T, so anyone wanting to use the name had to license it through AT&T. When AT&T sold its UNIX division to Novell in 1992, the UNIX name went to the X/Open foundation, who allowed any operating system to use the name UNIX that met certain specifications. Linux can't be called UNIX officially, since it has not gone through the X/OPEN specifications process. However, Linux can be called UNIX-like, UNIX-ish, or just plain Linux.

In 1981, IBM released their first home oriented computer, called the IBM PC. Since the early IBM PCs had a limited hardware architecture and ability to handle multiple users, it was not considered usable for the UNIX operating system. However, once the Intel 80286 came out, improved memory management and higher speeds allowed companies such as Microsoft (Xenix), Santa Cruz Organization (SCO UNIX), and Mark Williams Co. (Coherent) to start making versions of UNIX for the PC. One version that was developed was Minix. It was designed primarily to teach operating system design. There was little support for the 80386 functionality, some C compiler support, no networking, no X, and little support for multiple users.

In early 1991 Linus Torvalds, a student at the University of Helsinki, Finland, started work on a version of Minix that had support for things like virtual memory, multiple users, and used the 80386 instruction set. The idea of doing something more with this version took hold and he continued his work.

By September, Linus had version 0.01 and announced his project to other Minix users on the Internet. By January 1992, Linus had a system (version 0.12) that had a simple shell and C compiler. These were important because now Linus did not need to use Minix to recompile his operating system, which he named Linux as a play on his name. Additional tools, such as Internet support, additional programming tools, and the X-Window system came quickly as more and more users (and programmers) adopted Linux. The version numbers increased through version 0.99 in late 1993.

In early 1994, support for Linux was moving at a fast rate. Programmers from all over the world were writing code to support their particular hardware. Support for sound cards, CD-ROMs, video cards, mice, scanners, Ethernet cards, and just about every other kind of input/output device was being developed. In many cases, the support code was in 'beta' or test mode; sometimes it worked, and sometimes it had bugs. Some systems with particular hardware setups would work fine, and others would have problems. Around this time, a 'code freeze' was announced. The version of Linux at that point was 0.99pl15. This code freeze meant that no new functionality would be added, but old code would be fixed so it would work on almost every machine. The pl in the version number refers to patch level. A patch level is a minor correction in a release that isn't very large. A patch may fix something relatively minor such as a simple performance increase in a driver. A patch may also contain a major fix to an error.

Soon after this, version 1.0 of Linux was released. When versions of Linux are discussed, the number usually refers to the kernel itself instead of an entire installation. The 1.0 release was the most stable and most complete version available. As code changed to support more and more devices, the 1.1.x series was introduced. The 'odd' series as it is now known had the newest, yet least stable code in it. The 'even' series (1.0.x) had very stable, yet slightly older, code. As the 1.1.x series got more features and proved to be more stable, there was another code freeze, and 1.2.0 was released. Version 1.3.0 started off with even more added functionality.

This kernel release cycle continues: This allows sites to be able to have a stable and working system, while another site can take their chances and use the newest thing available. Right now, it is estimated that between 20,000 and a million machines throughout the world are using Linux. A Linux counter exists at http://domen.uninett.no:29659/request-form_eng.html which make estimates of the number of people registered versus the actual amount.

The GNU project allowed Linux to develop quickly. The GNU (which stands for GNU's Not Unix) project was started to develop a generic UNIX that would run on a variety of platforms. Since a UNIX system is more than just the kernel, the GNU project worked on developing free software for UNIX users. In order to avoid legal problems, or to differentiate their products from someone else's, the names of the programs for the UNIX counterparts have been changed. For example, the standard C compiler is usually called 'cc'. The GNU C compiler is called 'gcc' for 'Gnu CC.' To maintain compatibility, there are usually aliases or links between the old names and the new names so that you can still use the old names while really using the new products.

The GNU project also had a different concept on code ownership, called the GNU Copyleft. It bundled the ideas of public domain (everyone can own and modify the program) and freeware (a person owns the program, but allows everyone to use it for little or no cost). The basic idea of a program covered by the GNU Copyleft is as follows:

1.   The author still owns the program.

2.   Anyone can sell a copy of the program for any amount the market can bear, but there is no requirement to pay royalties to the original author.

3.   Anyone providing the software must also allow easy access to the original source code used to create the program.

Why Use Linux?

Linux is free. Like I said before, this is not necessarily free from monetary cost. You can still pay for Linux, and you can also pay to get Linux support from a number of consultants. The big thing is that you have the ability to change any piece of the kernel you like. If the output of a particular driver doesn't look right to you, you can change its output. If you think you can write a better memory management system, by all means go ahead and try it out. You can still take the one CD you purchased for $20 and give it to all your friends and co-workers and let them try Linux as well. The licensing of Linux allows an unlimited number of people to install from one CD-ROM.

Linux is stable. Both businesses and personal users need a stable system, and that is what Linux is. Stable in this sense means that it is less likely to crash than most other operating systems available for the PC. While some other operating systems crash once a day or once a week, many Linux users report in the range of months. The reasons for rebooting Linux systems is usually due to power outages, installing a new kernel, or installing new hardware.

Linux is complete. It's every bit the UNIX you'd expect to see from IBM, SCO, and Sun. All the utilities you'd expect to see are there, or there is a very close equivalent nearby. C compilers, Perl interpreters, shells of all sorts, and TCP/IP are all standard with Linux.

Linux is compatible. There is compatibility with SCO UNIX, so many applications that run under SCO UNIX can be used on Linux. There is a DOS emulator that will allow you to run many DOS-based applications. Work is also progressing on a Windows 3.1 emulator. Linux supports most PC hardware and drivers are being written for new hardware.

Linux is a full 32-bit operating system. A single process has the theoretical capability of accessing and using terabytes of memory. You don't have to worry about 640k code limits, using DOS extenders, EMM drivers, or loading drivers high, or . . . well you get the picture. Linux is 32 bits from the start.

Linux is configurable. It frees you from having to worry about 640k limits and performing memory optimizations every time you install a new driver. Linux gives you almost full control over how the system works. Imagine a windowing system where you can set the number of colors, resolution, and refresh to your specifications, instead of standard resolutions that make your eyes tired. You can have X running at a resolution of 900X650 if you like, or other combinations of resolutions. Many of the programs used to configure Linux can be changed on-the-fly without rebooting. The downside of this control is that there are a lot of files to edit. Once you get them fine-tuned however, little maintenance is required.

Linux works on many machines. If your machine doesn't have a lot of memory or doesn't seem quite as fast as the new machines coming out, that's okay. All Linux needs is an 80386 (SX or DX) based chip, 2MB of memory, and 10–20MB of disk space to start running. Of course, the more hardware you add, the faster Linux will be. For some small applications, such as handling e-mail for a small company, a low-end 486-based machine with 4MB or 8MB and a 120MB drive will work just fine. As this book is being written, work is progressing on ports of Linux to the Apple Macintosh, Sun, Dec Alpha, Amiga, and Power PC lines of computers.

Where to Get Linux

Distributions

Since Linux itself is not just the kernel, there has to be a way of getting together all the programs necessary for a full installation. These are called Linux Distributions, and many have appeared. Each distribution offers the same general tools, but with differences in the way the programs are installed, or in the way files are organized. In the end, each distribution will give you about the same thing after installation: a Linux system to work with. The following is a list of distributions:

1. *The Internet*. FTP sites carry distributions to get you started. Try ftp://sun-site.unc.edu/pub/Linux/distributions for a starting point.

2. *CD-ROM vendors*. If you don't feel like spending ten hours on a modem and using thirty diskettes to install a system, there are vendors at computer shows and in computer magazines that carry distributions of Linux. These CD-ROMs often contain 2 or more distributions, a complete copy of the

Linux software available at Linux FTP sites, plus some CD-ROMs containing a live filesystem. This allows you to install Linux on your machine without changing your current setup, try most of Linux out, and see if you like it. Only a small bit of your hard drive is taken up by Linux, which can be deleted from your system very easily. You can often test Linux using less than 20MB of space on a DOS drive.

3. *Prebuilt systems.* These vendors can build a system they guarantee will work with Linux and will usually install Dos/Windows or OS/2, if you wish to have that as well. These vendors are sometimes more expensive than buying the parts and installing Linux yourself, but many potential installation problems and conflicts are avoided.

4. *Commercial systems.* Companies like Flagship are bundling a version of Linux with their database software. Caldera is building an entire desktop out of Linux, complete with commercial applications such as Word Perfect.

One of the fastest ways to get information about Linux is through Usenet, the news service of the Internet. Many of the programmers of the original software regularly read the newsgroups and often help out with various problems. There are also others who probably had the same problem you did and can assist. As the saying goes: Two heads are better than one. I'm sure 500,000+ heads makes things a lot easier.

The Linux Journal, a monthly magazine reporting on the activities of Linux, contains a listing of consultants and companies who are offering Linux support for systems or software programming.

Linux Concepts versus DOS Concepts

When DOS was created (remember, UNIX is ten years older than DOS) it had a few features that existed in UNIX already which we will discuss here.

Kernel—This is something like the IBMDOS.SYS files that exist in DOS or the KRNL386.EXE file that exists for Windows. It sets up a lot of the low level routines and interacts directly with the CPU. In many cases, the user software doesn't interact with the CPU. The user program calls software functions that the kernel provides, then the kernel passes the instructions on to the CPU. The kernel also contains drivers for various kinds of hardware, much like a device file exists in the CONFIG.SYS file. In this way, the kernel provides two functions to the operating system:

1. It provides for a common interface to differing types of hardware. Each sound card looks (basically) the same way to user programs.

2.   It sets up 'barriers' between two different programs. If one program breaks, the other program won't be affected by it. A DOS system or Windows system can become unstable and not work properly since these barriers either don't exist or are not strong enough.

Shell—This is the way a user interacts indirectly with the kernel. In MS-DOS, the COMMAND.COM program is a shell. The shell is used to provide an easy interface for users to execute commands. Just as the COMMAND.COM can be replaced with another program (such as 4-DOS), the Linux shell can also be changed. The default shell is /bin/sh* or just sh. There are other shells available, such as tcsh, ksh, or zsh. With the exception of /bin/sh which has the lowest amount of functionality, much of the functionality is the same between the shells. Chapter 9 will cover the shells and how they work.

Multitasking—This is the ability of the operating system to give each program that is running use of the CPU. DOS does not do this, but Windows allows you to fake it. OS/2, NT, and Linux (UNIX) all have built-in support at the operating system level for multiple programs to be running at once. The kernel knows what programs (called processes in Linux's case) are in memory and tries to give each of them some CPU time. The kernel (really the job scheduler section of the kernel) will then balance tasks so that a more CPU-intensive process gets more time with the CPU. Say I'm using an editor, and I'm also running a ray trace. The kernel recognizes the fact that the ray trace is much more complicated than running the editor, so the ray tracer gets more CPU time than the editor. Since I (the user) am so much slower than the CPU, I don't notice it.

Multi-user—This is the ability to have multiple users accessing the same CPU at the same time. The CPU is running programs for multiple users concurrently, and the results are displayed on the remote display. Being multi-user means that I could be working at my PC, while a friend is logged in via a serial port from across the room, another dialed in through a modem, and a third logged in via Ethernet. This is not like a lan server, where the remote site (also known as a client) needs specific hardware and software setups. These remote users can have just about any kind of hardware setup. Each user is running their programs off the same CPU, and that CPU is handling all the users at once. A lan server (such as a Windows NT server or a Novell NetWare server) merely stores programs that can be run from the client CPU.

Process—Linux (and UNIX) uses what is known as processes. Each program that starts creates a process, which is a unique task in the eyes of the kernel. The

---

*   When programs are discussed, it usually gets referred to in terms of where the program is located on the drive.

terms process and program are sometimes interchangeable, but not always, as a program can start up many processes. DOS has the concept of processes but this is in the form of Terminate and Stay Resident (TSR) programs which merely load into memory and wait for an event. I'll go into processes a bit more in Chapter 2.

Super user—The super user, also known as the root account, is the one user who has full control over the system. Any file can be read, any directory changed. With this power comes great responsibility, as the root user has to (among other things)

Install software

Perform kernel upgrades

Perform backups

Attend to user issues

Fix small problems before they become big ones

Monitor the system to make sure resources (such as hard drive space) remain available to users

Handle networking issues.

Traditionally, the root account and the other accounts of the system were different people. Now that Linux gives you UNIX on your personal machine, you have to wear both of those hats. But don't worry. That's why you bought this book.

Users—The people who use the system are users. A username consists of eight characters or less and should be all lowercase. The username is related to a numeric UID (or User ID), which should be unique among usernames. This allows Linux to identify files and running programs.

Groups—A collection of users can be put together into a group. This allows for things like file ownership (see below) and provides a means for breaking down large groups of similar people. Group names also contain up to eight characters. As an example, a small college might want to break up users by majors:

compsci

chemeng

mecheng

techcomm

english

theater

This way, compsci users could share files and executable programs among other compsci users easily. As a further advantage, if the compsci students discover they need more hard drive space, the root user could assign a section of drive that is accessible to anyone in the compsci group. A single user can be in more than one group. For example, a person who has a double major in Computer Science and Technical Communication can be in the compsci and techcomm groups. This user will be able to access files from both groups.

File ownership—Since a Linux system has multiple users, there has to be a way for a user to protect his files from the prying eyes of another user, or if two users want to share information, but exclude others. Both of these situations can be dealt with by the way UNIX handles file ownership. There are three levels of permissions, and six levels of settings:

Levels:

Owner—This is the person who created the file

Group—The group that owns the file

Others—Anyone else not in the above two categories.

Settings:

Read—The ability to read or copy the file to another location

Write—The ability to edit or delete the file

Execute—The ability to run a program

SetUID—Run the program as another user

SetGID—Run the program as another group

Sticky—Prevents other users from deleting files in a directory.

A file can have its permissions set such that the user and anyone in the group can execute it, but no one else (except the root user) can read, write, or execute the program. In fact, you can change the permissions so that if you own the file, you can't read or write to it, but anyone else can. But since you own the file, you can change the permissions back so that you can read it.

The sticky bit is a somewhat special bit. Normally, when a directory is set to world writable, any user can delete any file in that directory regardless of the ownership or permissions of any file in that directory. A directory like /tmp needs to be world writable, since any user should be able to temporarily put files there. But having any user be able to delete files from /tmp could cause problems for other users. With the sticky bit set, the only files a user can delete in a world writable directory are ones owned by that user, or files that are also world writable.

CHAPTER 2

- Processes

- STDIN, STDOUT, and STDERR

- Pipes and Redirection

- Dynamically Linked Executables

- Drive Structure

- Directory Structure

- Special Files

- Compatibility with DOS, Windows, and OS/2

DOS vs. Linux

Processes

In DOS, once a program is loaded into memory, it is often rather hard to get it out of memory. This is because DOS stacks its programs in memory. If you load program A, then B, then C, DOS puts the programs such that A is buried beneath B and C. Removing program A requires removing programs B and C as well. Linux goes around this by allocating its memory in a way such that program A can be removed from memory without affecting B or C. MS Windows provides a similar capability. Its applications do not have to be closed in the order they were opened. You can close the windows anytime you like without a problem. Linux provides the added ability to easily signal a runaway process to be killed before it causes a problem.

In addition, Linux has the capability for swap space. Swap space is where a portion of the hard drive is used as virtual memory. While the hard drive is slower than RAM, processes that are inactive or waiting can be swapped out for a short amount of time by paging. A process gets cleared out of RAM and then stored in the swap memory, freeing up space for another process. When the process needs to use the CPU again, it gets swapped back into RAM where it resumes processing. However, too much paging at one time can cause thrashing, where the CPU is spending all of its time swapping memory to and from the hard drive, and no time is left for processes. Linux has some ability to prevent thrashing, but it can still occur. To prevent thrashing, make sure you have enough RAM. For a system that is not running X (one of Linux's windowing systems), 8MB should be enough with about 16MB of swap. For systems that do run X, 16MB and 16–32MB of swap should be okay.

MS-DOS   Linux

```
+----------------+      +----------------+
|                |      |                |
|   Program A    |      |   Process A    |
|                |      |                |
+----------------+      +----------------+
|                |      |                |
|   Program B    |      |                |
|                |      |   Free Space   |
+----------------+      |                |
|                |      |                |
|   Program C    |      +----------------+
|                |      |                |
+----------------+      |   Process B    |
|                |      +----------------+
|                |      |                |
|   Program D    |      |   Process D    |
|                |      +----------------+
+----------------+      |                |
|                |      |   Process C    |
|   Free Space   |      |                |
|                |      +----------------+
+----------------+
```

In order to remove program A under MS-DOS,
programs B, C, and D all have to be
removed from memory as well.
Linux can remove process A without changing
any other process.

MS-DOS   Linux

```
+----------------+      +----------------+
|                |      |                |
|                |      |   Free Space   |
|                |      |                |
|   Free Space   |      |                |
|                |      +----------------+
|  (but other    |      |                |
|  programs      |      |   Process B    |
|  were          |      |                |
|  stopped)      |      +----------------+
|                |      |                |
|                |      |   Process D    |
|                |      |                |
|                |      +----------------+
|                |      |                |
|                |      |   Process C    |
|                |      |                |
+----------------+      +----------------+
```

STDIN, STDOUT, and STDERR

STDIN refers to the standard input: the normal way a person interacts with a program. STDOUT is the way that normal programs send their output back to the user. STDERR is a special way of outputting such that it does not get caught in a pipe or redirection (see below) under normal circumstances. This way, if you get an unexpected but harmless error from a program, it will not corrupt the data that the next program is receiving.

Pipes and Redirection

Pipes and redirection exist in DOS. You may have already used a pipe or redirection if you have ever run either of the following commands:

```
more < file.txt
type file.txt | more
```

Pipes allow you to send the output of one program directly to the input of another program. Redirection allows you to use a file in place of STDIN, STDOUT, or STDERR. The above commands give the same output, but by two different means. In the first way, the file called `file.txt file` was used as standard input to the `more` command instead of being typed in from the keyboard. The second method uses the `type` command to read in the `file.txt` file, and send it out STDOUT to be picked up by the STDIN of more.

Dynamically Linked Executables

The MS Windows system has an idea similar to what exists in Linux, the Dynamically Linked Library. The idea is that you can make a smaller executable file by storing common C functions (such as `printf()`) in a central location where more than one process can use the function. There are a number of advantages to this:

1. The program's libraries can change easily. If the internal coding of a function like `printf()` changes, there is no need to recompile all your software. Just install the new library functions and continue to run your programs.

2. The executables take up less space. If you have 1000 programs that each take up 5k worth of C functions, that totals 5MB over the course of the 1000 files. If, however, you have one location for all the common C functions, it may take up 600k which contains more than the 5k of functions. Using the central location can save you over 4MB for that situation.

A program that has all the functions compiled in (which you can do if you like) is known as a statically linked file, since the libraries for the executable are static and will not change unless you recompile the program. A program that uses the common location strategy is known as dynamically linked, since the C functions it uses can change without you recompiling the software.

There are drawbacks to this dynamic linking system:

1. Executables start slower. Since the kernel has to load extra files to start a program, a dynamically linked program will take longer to load than a statically linked program.

2. Don't delete the libraries! If by accident, you delete the libraries that Linux uses, many of your programs will not work. Many of the programs rely on the libraries to work properly. To keep your Linux system somewhat usable in this event, some of the programs essential to running Linux have been statically linked, so that you can put the libraries back. These can usually be found in /sbin or /usr/sbin.

3. You had better have the libraries. There are cases when a program will need to use libraries you might not have installed yet. If you don't have the libraries, you'll have to either find the libraries or use a statically linked version of the program. This does not happen often, since most of the libraries you will need are included with your Linux distribution.

A new format for storing libraries is fast becoming popular, called ELF (for Executable Linking Format), and provides for a slightly smarter way of creating shared libraries. In the old format (called a.out), libraries had to be located in specific portions of memory. In order to prevent two libraries from coming into memory at the same location, a table was built and each library developer had to register their library. In addition, creating shared libraries was harder to do, as the developers needed to know memory locations and other information to place their libraries in the correct location. The ELF format allows the libraries to be placed anywhere in memory, which takes care of both the table and the memory programming. The down side is that programs have to be recompiled to use ELF. The a.out and ELF libraries can be in memory at the same time, but the two libraries are not directly compatible. There are also reports of anywhere between 5% loss to 5% gain in speed of running programs. If you have the option of loading an ELF-based version of Linux, take the ELF version.

Drive Structure

Linux stores its files such that there are no A: or C: drives that you may recognize from DOS or MS Windows.

From MS-DOS, you would first partition the drive using a program like FDISK to tell the drive how it should be split up. You would then use the FORMAT command to set that partition up for use in DOS. It would then be called a drive, such as the C drive or E drive and so on.

In Linux, you still partition the physical drive to separate it out. Then, you use a program like mke2fs to format the partition, which is now called a filesystem.

The users deal with only one drive, and everything is shown in terms of subdirectories of that drive to the user. Since there has to be a root directory, one that everything mounts off of, Linux provides a root directory, called /.

You could have one filesystem for the root directory and other files (the / directory), another filesystem for user commands (the /usr directory) and another filesystem for user space (the /home or /user directory). For example, I have three partitions that I use: One is for the / directory, one is for the /usr directory, and the third one is for the /home directory.

When Linux boots, it mounts the root directory, then all other filesystems are mounted off the root directory. In my case, /usr would get mounted then /home. I could also have directories such as /usr/X11R6, which contains the X-Window System program files, on a separate partition and be mounted off of /usr. Of course, I would need /usr mounted first for this to work successfully.

When I use the cd command to change directories, it is just like using cd from DOS to change to a subdirectory. The only difference is that I do not have to switch drive letters. I just use cd and Linux will move me to the right filesystem.

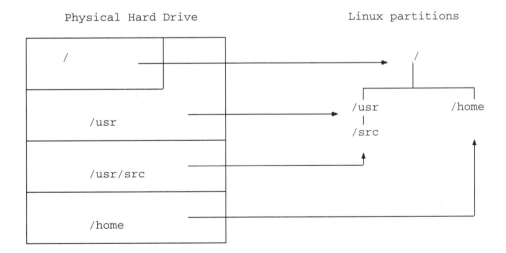

Hard drive partitions can be mounted just about anywhere in the Linux system

There are a few advantages to using this system. First, you can add more total space to the system by adding partitions. If you notice that the /usr/X11R6 sub-directory will take up more space than /usr has, you can create a new filesystem. This new filesystem could be created from the unused portion of a drive, or from a new drive. You can then mount the new partition as /usr/X11R6. Second, most changes in partition are invisible to both the user and the user's programs. DOS needs a drive letter and a directory. Linux just needs a directory, and, in many cases, the program will not notice if you use a file on another partition.

Linux refers to physical drives, such as the 3.5" floppy drive, as special files located in the /dev directory. For example, the first drive (called A: in DOS) is called /dev/fd0 in Linux. The fd refers to the fact that it is a floppy drive, and the 0 means that it is the first of that kind of device.

Hard drives are referred to in two different ways: the physical drive itself and by a partition on that physical drive. Hard drive entries in /dev are prefixes with hd to signify hard drive. It is followed by an 'a' for the first physical drive, a 'b' for the second physical drive, and so on. Remember this refers to the physical drive. After that is a number to specify the partition within the physical drive. The first partition is 1, the second partition is 2, and so on.

SCSI devices follow hard drive format, only their prefix is sd instead of hd. The sd means SCSI drive, since a Linux machine can have both IDE and SCSI drives.

In order to help you think in Linux, here are a few translations of a DOS drive and its Linux counterpart:

DOS		LINUX
A:		/dev/fd0
B:		/dev/fd1
C:	(assuming first partition on the first hard drive)	/dev/hda1
E:	(assuming second partition on the second hard drive)	/dev/hdb2

Directory Structure

In order for programs to work together, a directory structure was set up that most users should follow. This allows programs to know where certain files are, and allows different vendors to provide installations that won't conflict with other vendor's installations. The FSSTND project (for File System Standard) is a group of Linux users who are defining what files should go in what directories and how the directories should be set up. Many CD-ROM vendors already follow this standard, and your installation probably follows this setup rather closely.

Here are a few of the suggestions from the FSSTND group for directories and what they contain:

`/etc`	machine-local system configuration
`/usr/bin`	most user commands
`/dev`	device files
`/usr/man`	on-line manuals
`/usr/include`	standard `include` files for C
`/var/log`	system logging and user accounting files
`/home`	user directories
`/usr/local`	extra programs not part of a usual system /usr/local has some additional directories under it:

```
                           /usr/local/bin
                           /usr/local/man
                           /usr/local/lib
                           /usr/local/include
```

`/usr/src`	location for source code (including the Linux source code)
`/usr/lib`	library files for user programs.

Special Files

There are five major file types that can exist on a drive (also known as a filesystem). The types are file, directory, link, named pipe, and device file. The file and directory types you probably already know. Files can contain executable programs, data files, e-mail, and other forms of information. Directories contain these files.

Link

DOS has commands like `subst` and `join` which can make a directory appear as a separate drive to the operating system. If you used join to make the `C:\FILES\TXT\1995\JAN\WEEK1` directory look like the Q drive, then typed `dir q:` you would see what is really in the directory on the C drive. Linux takes this a few steps further by allowing a file to exist in one directory while it really exists in another directory. To understand this, you have to understand that the way Linux stores files is similar to the way the FAT for MS-DOS looks at files. Each file has a directory entry, and a special identifier called an inode. This inode is a unique pointer for the system to find a file within a directory.

Here is an example to show how links work in the GNU gzip program. Gzip compresses the size of a file much the same way a program like pkzip does. DOS would require you to do one of two things. First, you could have two programs—one for compressing and one for decompressing. Since much of the code is similar, this is a waste of space. The other option is to have some run-time configuration of the program, where the user can type gzip -c to compress, and gzip -d to decompress. While this saves some space, it requires the user to remember the swiches. Wouldn't it be easier to have two programs, one called gzip and the other called gunzip, which really executed the same code?

Gzip comes as one file, called gzip. From here, you create a link to a file called gunzip. Now you have two programs with the same data, but called by different names. The gzip program is told how you called the program, so if you typed gzip text.txt, the compression portions of the code would activate. The same goes for if you ran gunzip text.txt.gz. The internal code would recognize that you typed gunzip instead of gzip and would start the decompression portion of the code.

Another example comes from a CD-ROM Linux installation. Since you may not use all of the programs in a standard installation, your installation creates links from where Linux expects the file to be to where the file actually resides on the CD-ROM. The benefit is that instead of having a 500k file which you may not use often, you have a 12 byte file.

There are two kinds of links: hard and soft. A soft link creates a new inode for the new file, but points to the inode of the original program. Since they point to the same file, if you edit (or delete or whatever) one file, the other one is changed in exactly the same manner, since they are pretty much the same file.

Be aware that deleting a link destination does not make the links to the file disappear. The links will still be there, and you will get a 'file not found' error if you try to access it.

A hard link actually creates a new file, but gives that file the same inode as the original file. The difference between this and a soft link is that if one of the linked files is deleted, the other links will still remain. The file will not really be deleted until all of the links to that file are deleted.

There are a few limitations on what can be hard linked. You cannot make a hard link across filesystems, since inodes are different across filesystems. That is, if you had two partitions, one mounted on /home and the other on /usr, you

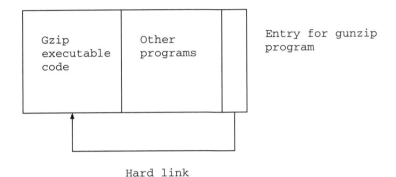

Hard link

Executing gunzip really activates the code for gzip, since the code shares the same space on the physical drive.

would not be able to make a hard link from /home to /usr. You also can't hard link directories. You would have to use soft links in these situations.

The ln command is used to make links.

```
ln -s <source> <destination>
```

will create a soft link from the source to the destination file.

```
ln <source> <destination>
```

will create a hard link between the two files.

You can tell what kind of link is to a file by looking at the directory entry of the file.

If you use ls -l to look at a file that has hard links, you'll see the following:

```
> ls -l g*
-rwxr-xr-x  3 root    root     45277 Aug 20 18:25 gunzip
-rwxr-xr-x  3 root    root     45277 Aug 20 18:25 gzip
```

To the left of the first root you see a 3. This means that there are three hard links. The third file is zcat, a program that uncompresses a file and sends it directly to the screen. If one of the links were to be deleted (say zcat), then the entry would look like this:

```
> ls -l g*
-rwxr-xr-x  2 root    root     45277 Aug 20 18:25 gunzip
-rwxr-xr-x  2 root    root     45277 Aug 20 18:25 gzip
>
```

You may notice that directories may look like they have hard links as well. This is somewhat true, since the number tells you how many subdirectories are in that directory.

A soft link can be discovered by the name in the directory. The tcsh shell is a shell that is a replacement for the csh shell. In order to do this, a soft link is made from csh to tcsh:

```
> ls -l csh tcsh
lrwxrwxrwx  1 root    root             4 Oct 13 15:56 csh -> tcsh
-rwxrwxr-x  1 root    root        252496 Sep  6 12:52 tcsh
>
```

You can see in the csh entry that there is a kind of arrow after it. This signifies that it is a soft link to the tcsh program.

Pipes

A named pipe (also called a FIFO for First In, First Out) allows you to pass data from one process to another. Using the `mkfifo` command, you can create a named pipe:

```
> mkfifo pipe
```

Then you can set up two processes. One that writes to the file, and another that reads from it.

We'll call this window one:

```
> cat < pipe
```

And this window two:

```
> cat > pipe
```

At this point, anything you type in window two gets displayed on window one. Ending the data flow (by pressing CTRL-C or CTRL-D on window one) will end both programs. This can also be done with regular files, only pipes don't store what you type in. The resulting file size of the pipe file is 0.

Devices

Linux handles its physical devices (such as the hard drive) in a way that is easier to understand, but harder to use. In order to access these devices, Linux uses the device file type. The devices are commonly stored in the `/dev` directory, and their `ls -l` entry looks like this:

```
brw-rw-rw-  1 root    root     2,   0 Dec 31 1979 fd0
crw-w--w-   1 root    root     4,   0 Mar 13 1994 tty1
```

The `tty1` filename refers to the first available tty device, the one that you see when Linux boots. There are tty devices, hd devices (for the hard drive), ttyS devices (to use the serial ports), fd devices (for the floppy drives), and the pty ports which are for users logged in via TCP/IP.

The c all the way on the left side means it is a character device file. In this case, the file refers to the tty, or teletype, device. The fd0 (for the first floppy drive) has a b because it's a block device. A chararacter device handles data in sets of characters, one at a time. A block device file can handle a block of data at once. A floppy drive can write an entire block of data at once, while a serial port or a tty handles data one character at a time.

The tty is the common way that a user will enter input to Linux. Devices have two special numbers to the left of the date; in our example, the 4 and the 0. The 4 refers to the major number of the device, and the 0 refers to the minor number of the device. The major number is usually for big classes of devices. The floppy drives have a major number of 2, the hard drive has a major number of 3, and so on. The tty series of devices has a major number of 4. The minor number refers to a subdivision of the major device. Since there are nine tty devices, one for each Virtual Console that Linux has, the minor numbers range from 0 to 8. For floppy drives, the minor number refers to the drive type. The primary floppy drive that is a high density drive, but has a low density 3.5" diskette in it, has a minor number of 16, while a high density drive with a high density 3.5" diskette in it has a minor number of 28. Don't worry about the major and minor numbers, as you rarely need to use them. For almost all installations, the /dev directory will be set up for you already. If not, a program called MAKEDEV may be available to create many of the device files for you.

There are two ways to access these devices. First, you can write a program which activates the port using a C function call. This allows you a great amount of control over the port. The downside of this, of course, is that you have to write a C program to do it. The second way is to send files to it using redirection. For example, if you had an audio file, you could listen to it like this:

```
cat sound.au > /dev/audio
```

and you'll hear the sound come out of the speakers.

Login Shell

The Linux shell provides most of the functionality needed to interact with the system. It has many of the same things that the DOS COMMAND.COM does, including:

1. Environment variables—Variables that may be specific to each user or even each login of a particular user. This includes the search path for finding executable programs

2.   Programs to run at startup—The AUTOEXEC.BAT file or the STARTUP group in Windows

3.   The prompt the user sees—The prompt pg that you are probably familiar with from DOS.

In addition to this, the shell provides even more capablilites:

1.   Set the terminal type—Linux can't make assumptions about the kind of terminal you are using, since you can log in from a Sun workstation, the console, a Windows telnet program, or through a teletype attached to a modem. One of the things the shell tries to do is determine what kind of terminal you are using.

2.   Set various keys to perform certain functions (like backspace)—There are really two commands you can use for backspace: backspace and delete. Even if the shell knows what kind of terminal you are using, it doesn't know what you use to erase a previous character, so the shell sets this for you, and various other commands for job control get set up as well.

The default shell for UNIX is /bin/sh. Linux uses a version called /bin/bash (for Bourne Again Shell). Bash is one of the lowest level shells you'll find for Linux. Other shells like csh or ksh or zsh all provide different functionality that bash lacks. Bash does provide the following:

1.   Built in aliasing—You can set up aliases so that you can run one program, or a program with your favorite switches, as a different name. I have dir aliased to ls -l so that if I type dir to the shell, the shell actually executes ls -l. Again, DOSKEY performs some of this functionality.

2.   Job control—This is the ability of the shell to run more than one process at a time, and let the user control each one. Chapter 4 covers job control.

3.   Low memory usage—Linux provides the ability to share memory across processes. This allows two similar processes to use the same memory. For example, one shell running may take up 300k, but starting a second shell may only add 200k to what is being used.

Compatability with DOS, Windows, and OS/2

Linux provides the capability to access your DOS and OS/2 drives even though DOS or OS/2 isn't running. Accessing your DOS (also known as FAT—for File Allocation Table) drives is as easy as using the mtools package, which you'll read about in a later chapter. There is also a DOS emulator which will run most programs, including Windows. There is a Windows emulator in the works, called WINE. Once completed, WINE will allow you to run Windows applications from within the X-Window System at speeds equal to or greater than a machine running MS Windows.

X-Windowing System

The X-Windowing System is a way to provide a graphical user interface (GUI) system to an operating system. X is a bit harder to use than Microsoft Windows, but X provides you with much greater control and configurability. Plus you can get the source code for X and compile your own version of it if you like.

Networking

Linux has compatability not only with TCP/IP, the main protocol used on the Internet, but other networking protocols as well:

Lan Manager   used by Windows for Workgroups
                 Windows 95, and Windows NT among others

IPX   used by NetWare

AppleTalk   used by MacOS

This allows you to easily add a Linux machine to most networks.

CHAPTER 3

Using
the System

Logging In

By now you should have Linux installed and working fine. If not, follow the instructions for your particular setup and get Linux installed. Covering the multitude of configuration issues would fill another book, and most of these issues will be covered by your particular Linux installation software.

Here's where you get to log in and look around. Unlike DOS, Windows, and OS/2, UNIX has multiple users accessing the same CPU at the same time. To separate these users, each user is assigned four things to make sure that each user's program is unique:

1. UID—This is the UserID which is a number between 0 and 32767. The only all powerful UID is 0 which is defined as the root account, or super user. Any user who has the UID of 0 has the most control over the system.

2. Username—This is a way of mapping a UID to something a bit more meaningful. The username is a name of eight characters or less given to that user. You can create this username in any way that you like. Traditionally, the username with UID 0 (the super user) is called 'root,' however, there is no requirement that you do this. As a security note, two usernames can have the same UID; that is, root can be UID 0, and an account called bob can have a UID of 0. This means that the bob and root accounts are each considered the superuser.

3. GID—Group ID defines which logical group the user belongs to. The group ID won't prevent you from running most programs.

4. Groupname—A name that represents the GID. It has eight or less characters.

When logging into Linux, you must provide two things. First you must provide your username. This is the way of telling Linux who you are. The second thing you must give is a password. The password is Linux's way of verifying that you have permission to use that account.

In UNIX, passwords, usernames, and other account information is usually stored in the /etc/passwd file. While any user may read this file, the passwords stored in this file are encrypted to prevent anyone else from learning your password. There are alternate methods of storing the passwords available to Linux such as the shadow password system. The shadow password stores passwords in a file readable only by root, decreasing the chances that someone can break into the system.

Behind the scenes, before you log in, are two programs. First is the getty process. It continually runs on all possible login devices. For example, it monitors the keyboard to see if anyone is using it. Getty can also monitor a serial port or modem for activity. Once getty receives a signal that someone wants to log in (either because someone typed in a username, or the modem picked up the phone), it turns control over to the /bin/login program, which actually picks up the username and gets the password. The password is then encrypted and checked against the encrypted password entry in the /etc/passwd file. If the passwords don't match, the user has to re-enter the username and password. If the passwords do match, control is passed to the login shell, usually /bin/bash. At this point, the user is logged in. Control of that port will stay with the shell until you get disconnected (the phone line goes dead on a modem for instance) or you intentionally log out (by typing exit or logout).

The first thing you should do is log in as root, change root's password, then create a regular user for yourself. Why? The root user has too much power. It is too easy to type a command which could delete a good portion of your system. If you have a user which has normal priveleges, the chances of major problems go down. So let's log you in and create a user.

```
Welcome to Linux 1.2.1.

login:
```

Here is where you'll want to log in as root. Just type 'root' and hit the enter key.

```
Welcome to Linux 1.2.1.

login: root
bash#
```

You were able to log in without a password. Linux uses passwords in order to prevent other users from logging in as you. On the first installation of most Linux systems, the root account is left blank so that you are able to log in and start using the system. If you are asked for a password, use the one provided with your system.

You should set a password for yourself using the `passwd` command. Even though the password is encrypted, using bad passwords makes it easier for someone to crack into your system. There are suggestions for passwords in Chapter 13. Even if you don't plan on allowing anyone else to log in, it's still a good idea to put passwords on the root account.

```
bash# passwd
Changing password for root
New Password: <type in your password here>
Re-enter new password: <type it in again>
Password changed
bash#
```

The reason that passwd prompted you twice in this example was to make sure you typed it in right the first time. If there was a difference in the passwords, you would have to go through the procedure of typing in the password twice again. This protects you from mistyping the password, and not knowing how it was misspelled. If this happened, you wouldn't be able to access your account again. If it does happen, you'll need to go through quite a bit of trouble to boot the system from your boot and root floppies, mount your root device, and edit the `/etc/passwd` file so that the root user doesn't have a password again.

Virtual Consoles

Linux has a helpful feature when you're at the console. Pressing ALT-F2 will bring up a new login screen. Pressing ALT-F1 returns you to your original screen. This is what's known as virtual consoles, since you can have more than one console active at a time. The default is usually to have about six virtual consoles that you can log into. Because these are virtual consoles, you can usually switch between consoles, even when running a VGA application or X. This allows you to run multiple programs at once without running X. This is good for systems that have a slower CPU or not enough memory to run X.

Not all UNIX implementations have this, so you may not see it everywhere. A few other PC-based UNIX systems (both free and commercial) support virtual consoles.

Creating Users

To create users in Linux, use the `useradd` command. There are three commands that the root user can use to manipulate users: `useradd`, `usermod`, and `userdel`, which create, modify, and delete user accounts. The root user (or anyone who has a UID of 0) is the only user that can modify, create, or delete accounts.

To start out, there is not much you need to know about `useradd`, only enough to create a user. Let's say you wanted to create an account named `mark`:

```
bash# useradd -g users -m mark
bash# passwd mark
New Password: <enter a password>
Re-type new password: <enter it again>
bash#
```

It doesn't look like anything happened, but something did. Logout (type `exit` or `logout`), then when you're at the login prompt, enter the new account you just created:

```
Welcome to linux 1.2.1.
login: mark
password: <enter your password>
Linux 1.2.0. (Posix).
trippy:~$
```

Now you have your user account to explore UNIX. Now on to the first thing you see, the prompt:

```
trippy:~$
```

The first bit that says 'trippy', is the name of the system that I'm logged into. The colon is there as a separator. The ~ tells you which directory you are in. In this case, the ~ represents the home directory for the `mark` account. The $ is also a separator. Just as DOS has an environment variable for setting the prompt (set prompt=pg), so does the bash shell. You may have noticed that when you logged in as root above, the prompt looked quite different. The end of the prompt was a # instead of a $. The sh prompt for the root user is a # instead of a $. Why? Think of it as a reminder that you are logged in as root and to be careful of what you're doing.

How to Get Help

Some of the commands you will be using have a quick help switch. For example, for help on the `ls` command, you can type:

```
trippy:~$ ls —help
```

You'll get a quick summary of what the command does. In some cases, such as with `ls`, the help spans more than one screen. In this case, you may want to pipe the information through the `more` command:

```
trippy:~$ ls —help | more
```

To get more in-depth help, you can use the `man` command.

The man program gives you access to all the manual pages that are available on the system. You can get help on just about any command or C function, and many configuration files can also be found. To use `man`, just type `man <command name>` and you'll see a screen like this:

```
man(1)                                  man(1)

NAME
     man—format and display the on-line manual pages
     manpath—determine user's search path for man-pages

SYNOPSIS
     man [-adfhktw] [-m system] [-p string] [-C config_file]
     [-M path] [-P pager] [-S section_list] [section] name ...

DESCRIPTION
     man formats and displays the on-line manual pages. This
     version knows about the MANPATH and PAGER environment
     variables, so you can have your own set(s) of personal man-
     pages and choose whatever program you like to display the
     formatted pages. If section is specified, man only looks
     in that section of the manual. You may also specify the
     order to search the sections for entries and which prepro-
     cessors to run on the source files via command line
     options or environment variables. If name contains a /
     then it is first tried as a filename, so that you can do
     man ./foo.5 or even man /cd/foo/bar.1.gz.
```

The man pages are set up in a fairly standard way. The top line of each page has the name followed by the command's section number. The next few lines have the command and any others that might share functionality, along with a quick description of what the program does. In the case of man, there are two programs here: `man` and `manpath`.

After that, the page contains ways the program can be run. First is the command name, followed by required options. These are options that are needed by the program to run correctly. Anything in square brackets is optional.

Further down is a somewhat longer explanation of the program and how it works, followed by a listing of the command line options and how they work.

Near the end can be any of a number of things, but you may see a section on potential bugs, who wrote the software, and any associated man pages that involve this program that would have more information.

Man itself has a man page, since there are many different options. Here are a few of them:

<number>—The man pages are set up in a way such that there are nine sections of documentation. This allows you to have a few different copies of documentation for a program, where one would be of interest to general users, while a system administrator might be given extra options.

The groups are as follows:

1—General user programs
2—System C calls
3—User C calls
4—Special files (devices)
5—File formats
6—Games
7—Miscellaneous
8—System Administration utilities
9—Kernel internal variables and functions

Man will search starting with section 1 and continue until it gets past section 9. If it finds a man-page it will display the manual page for the page, otherwise you will get, a No manual entry for <command> message.

The only time you really need to use the chapter number is if what you're looking for appears twice and you want the second instance. For example, write has more than one entry in the man pages. The first instance, write(1), is used to communicate with other users. The second instance, write(2) , is a C function called to write a file. Entering

```
man write
```

will only give you the first instance of write. To get the second, you'd have to type

```
man 2 write
```

or use the -a option (see below).

-k <keyword>—You can do a search on a keyword. Each of the man-pages can be configured so that an index of the commands and quick explanations of the command are created. Using the -k option allows you to search that index. The makewhatis command will build this index for you. Another command that does the same thing is whatis and apropos.

The man program uses the `more` command to give you a page full of text at a time. To scroll to the next screen, hit the space bar. To quit, you can type q. You can get help for more by typing h while viewing a manual page or another text file via `more`.

-a—This will return all the entries that `man` finds, not just the first. In the case of `write`, which has two entries in the man database, you would first get write(1), then write(2).

How to Get Out

Don't you hate getting into something, and not knowing how to get out of it? So do I. I'll tell you three things you can do to get out:

1. *Log out but leave Linux running*—get to a shell prompt (so that you see the $ or a #) and type `exit` or `logout`. Getting to the shell prompt will require that you leave the command you're currently running. With the `more` command or from the manual pages, you can type q. Linux is still running, but once you exit the system, you have no interaction with the system until you log in again.

   Shutting down the Linux system is not as easy as turning off the PC as you could with DOS. Since Linux is running many things at once, many files may be open, and turning off the PC without shutting down Linux properly can corrupt those files. There are two ways of shutting down Linux properly. You have to be logged in as root to do either of these functions.

2. *Reboot the machine*—This will be the same as if you hit the Control-Alt-Delete in DOS. All you need to do is log in as the root user and type `reboot`. The Linux system will shut itself down, then automatically reboot. It's a good idea to have other programs shut down and all the other users logged off.

3. *Stop the machine*—This does the same as reboot, except the machine halts. All processes are stopped, and all the filesystems are unmounted. Log in as the root user and type `halt`. Linux will shut down all of its running programs, then leave a message telling you:

```
It is now safe to turn off the power.
```

or

```
The system is halted.
```

You can also schedule times for shutting down using the `shutdown` command. The syntax is

```
shutdown <time> <message>
```

where `<time>` is the time to be shutdown. I can be in a few formats, including hh:mm for the actual hour and minute to shutdown (11:30 for 11:30 A.M. for example). Another format is the number of minutes from now to shutdown using the `+<s>` option, in which case it will wait `<s>` minutes. The special time now means to shutdown immediately, and is the same as saying +0.

The `<message>` is what will get sent to the users of the system just before the shutdown occurs. For example, the command

```
shutdown +30 "The system is going down to upgrade the kernel"
```

will shut the machine down in thirty minutes with the message broadcast to all users.

The shutdown command by itself brings the system into what is called single user mode. In this mode, all filesystems except for root are unmounted, all users except root are removed from the system, and all other programs (including networking) are terminated. You can change this behavior by using one of two options. The `-h` flag makes shutdown behave as if it was halt, and `-r` makes shutdown act as the reboot command.

DOS	Linux	Function
help	man	get help on a command
type	cat	list a file to the screen
more	more	list a file a page at a time
dir	ls	directory listing
cd	cd	change directory
mkdir (or md)	mkdir	make directory
rmdir (or rd)	rmdir	remove directory
del	rm	remove a file
edit	vi (or emacs)	edit a file
attrib	chmod	modify a file permissions
copy	cp	copy a file
move	mv	move a file (copy, then delete)
himem	**	XMS memory
emm386	**	EMS memory
memmaker	**	Optimize memory usage
smartdrv	**	Disk caching

Any Linux entries with '**' means that either the kernel does it, or is otherwise not needed by Linux.

Using the System

Many of the commands available under Linux are much the same as their DOS or OS/2 counterparts. See table on page 32 for a listing of some of the more familiar DOS commands and the commands under Linux.

One function of the shell is making aliases, so that if you prefer using `del` instead of `rm`, you only have to type

```
trippy:~> alias del='rm'
trippy:~>
```

and for as long as you are logged in, anytime you type `del` the shell will really run `rm`. You also have the ability to load aliases when you login via the `.cshrc` and `.login` files.

CHAPTER
4

- Redirects

- Pipes

- STDIN, STDOUT, STDERR, and Redirection

- Job Control

- Background Jobs and STDIN

The Linux Environment

Redirects

Redirection is a way of using a file in place of the monitor or the keyboard. What usually gets written to the screen goes into a file (STDOUT), and what usually gets entered from the keyboard gets entered from a file (STDIN). The advantage is that programs do not need a lot of extra code to use STDIN and STDOUT. This is because it's a part of the shell, which is really between the program and the user. There are many applications that use this. For example, a directory listing that fills the screen can be captured to a file and printed out later. In this case, you would take the output of one command, which is `ls` and send what that program would normally output directly to a file. You don't see what the output is, but you can examine the file later and confirm that the output is right. Redirection works in a similar way, using a file to replace what you would normally type in. One use of this is the `more` command. You can use the command `more < file` and the input that `more` expects comes from the file. If you wanted a file that contains a directory listing along with a line at the end that shows the date you make the file, you can't do this:

```
trippy:~> ls > file
trippy:~> date > file
```

The output of this procedure is only the date:

```
Wed Mar 15 21:08:45 EST 1995
```

You may also get an error out of this, such as `"file: File exists"`. If so, type `set noclobber` and try again. Some shells have a feature you can set that prevents you from accidentally overwriting a file.

When you use > to send output to a file, the shell will overwrite the file with the new data coming in. To prevent this, use >> instead. This means append to the end of the file. So, you would use

```
trippy:~> ls > file
trippy:~> date >> file
```

and the date would be the last line in the file.

Pipes

Pipes work as both redirections at once. Pipes take the output of one program and send it as input to another. Note the following command:

```
trippy:~> ls | more
```

It does the same thing as

```
trippy:~> ls > dir.tmp
trippy:~> more < dir.tmp
```

The output of the ls command gets sent to the more program as input. This way, you don't have to worry about creating or keeping track of temporary files. When using the pipe method, the temporary files do not appear.

STDIN, STDOUT, STDERR, and Redirection

Imagine a case where you use a pipe to move data between two programs, and the first program (the one sending the data to the second one) finds an error. Should it simply print a message to the screen? The answer is no, because the error message would get caught by the pipe (or redirection) and two things would happen:

1. The user would never see the error message. How good is an error message if you can't find it?

2. The program that is receiving data from the first could get confused finding an error message among the data it is expecting and could possibly corrupt the second program. This is definately the more serious of the two consequences, and as later chapters show, there are a lot of cases where pipes are used.

To solve this, there is a special output called STDERR which does not go through the normal redirection of > and >>, but instead gets sent directly to the user's screen as if there was no redirection. This lets you see an error or warning immediately, without corrupting the current process(es).

To use STDIN, STDOUT, and STDERR, some shells use magic numbers to tell what should get redirected. These numbers usually are

`0: STDIN`

`1: STDOUT`

`2: STDERR`

To show how redirection works, I'll introduce you to another switch to the `ls` command, the R switch. The R means to 'recurse' or to try and get a directory of each directory under it, and each directory under that, and so on until it is out of directories. Let's say we have our directory structure set up like this:

```
/home/mark-
          |
          |-Mail
          |-News
          |-locked
          |-unlocked
              |-directory
```

Let's say that I don't have any permission for 'locked' (so that even I as the file owner do not have read, write, or execute permissions on the directory). If I were to type `ls -lR > file`, instead of getting my shell prompt back, I would see

```
trippy:~> ls -lR > file.txt
ls: locked: Permission denied
trippy:~>
```

If you look through the `file.txt` file, you will not find this error message. The only hint of an error is what you see on the screen, along with the fact that you don't see what is in the `locked` directory, while you can see what is in the `Mail`, `News`, `unlocked`, and `unlocked/directory` directories.

There are ways of capturing the STDERR output, however. The bash shell allows you to capture STDERR in a way similar to redirecting STDOUT. The difference being that you preface the > with a '2'. So, to capture all regular output from our above `ls` command to file, and all errors to `err.file`, we would have

```
trippy:~> ls -lR > file 2> err.file
trippy:~>
```

And if we look at the `err.file`, we see

```
trippy:~> cat err.file
ls: locked: Permission denied
trippy:~>
```

But the output of the `ls -lR` command still exists in the file without the error message.

To have even more fun, there is a file in the Linux system called `/dev/null`, which represents a bit bucket. You can't read anything from this file, but any data sent to it is effectively erased. If we never wanted to see the error in the first place, then we could write this:

```
trippy:~> ls -lR > file 2> /dev/null
trippy:~>
```

and you would not see any errors sent to the screen.

Job Control

The shell has the ability to let Linux take a command and run with it while you go off and do something else with the shell. Doing this is called backgrounding a process. This involves Linux (the shell really) taking the process that you just typed in, running it, disconnecting STDIN from that process, and giving control of the terminal back to the shell. STDOUT is still connected (unless you redirect it). To put a process in the background, just add an ampersand (&) to the end of your command line:

```
trippy:~> ls &
[1] 118
trippy:~> FILE1                      FILE2
FILE3                  FILE4
[1]     Done                 ls
trippy:~>
```

Let's back up and see what happened above. The `ls &` specifies to the shell that we want to run the `ls` program in the background. The next line has a `[1]` which means it's the first background job that this shell is working on. The `118` is the process number. The process number is a unique identification number for each process that Linux is currently running. It's one of the ways that Linux tracks processes. Then we get our prompt back. But before we do anything (since `ls` isn't a very cpu intensive program to run) we get output on STDOUT. STDOUT was never redirected, so `ls` can still write to it. The output comes out; in this case, there are four files that get listed. The second to last line is the `[1]` to tell us that we're talking about the first background job, then a status on it (Done), and the command that was running, just in case we forgot.

In some shells, there is a way of putting a job in the background interactively. That is, a program that is running can be put into the background so that you can do other work. You can usually do this by pressing CTRL-Z (or ^Z). By default, this is the key that the shell is looking for to signal that you want to suspend (or pause) a running process. So, going back to the ls example, say we have a lot of files in that directory, and we want to redirect the output to a file. If we typed:

```
trippy:~> ls /home/mark/bigdirectory > /home/mark/bigdirlisting
```

it might take us a few seconds to get a prompt back. While this process is running, we could hit the CTRL-Z key and get the shell back:

```
trippy:~> ls /home/mark/bigdirectory > /home/mark/bigdirlisting
```
(here we hit ^Z)

```
Suspended
```

```
trippy:~>
```

So right now, the job is not running at all. As far as Linux is concerned, it's suspended. From here, we could do any of four things:

1. Bring the job back to the foreground.

2. Put the job in the background.

3. Kill the job.

4. Leave the process as it is.

Option 1 would be the same as if we did not hit ^Z to begin with. The process would resume, and the prompt would not return until the job was completed. To do this, we would type the following:

```
trippy:~> fg
```

```
For ForeGround.
```

Option 2 would treat the process as if we included an ampersand at the end of the command. To do this, just type bg. The process would resume running in the background, and we would regain immediate control of the shell. We would see this:

```
trippy:~> bg
[1]   ls /home/mark/bigdirdirectory > /home/mark/bigdirlisting &
trippy:~>
[1]    Done                    ls /home/mark/bigdirdirectory >
/home/mark/bigdirlisting &
trippy:~>
```

This is just as if the process was put in the background to begin with. At any point, you can bring the job to the foreground again by typing `fg`.

Option 3 would kill the job altogether. The process would be ended, memory cleared, and immediate control of the shell would return. To kill the job, we would type

```
trippy:~> kill %1
```

The `%1` in this case refers to the first job that is controlled by the shell. If the shell is controlling more than one job at a time (say you have two processes running in the background) then you would have %2 or %3 or %n, where n is the job number.

While kill requires using the %1 or %2 or %3, using this for `fg` or `bg` is optional. If you use `bg` or `fg` without a parameter, it defaults to the most recently accessed process. That is, if you have three jobs running on the same shell, and you brought job #2 to the foreground with `fg %2` then typed `bg`, that second job would resume running in the background. In some cases, you can also enter just 2 instead of `%2`.

Option 4 just leaves the process as it is—suspended for an indefinite amount of time. You can restart it, kill it, or pop it in the background at a later time.

To get a listing of the jobs and the status of each of the shell's jobs, use the `jobs` command.

```
trippy:~> jobs
[1]  + Suspended          ls
[2]    Running            ls > ~/fubar
trippy:~>
```

We see here that job #2 is running, and job #1 has been suspended. Don't worry about accidentally logging off before a particular job finishes. If you try to log out before a job is completed, the shell will respond with

```
trippy:~> logout
There are stopped jobs.
trippy:~>
```

If you type `logout` again, the shell will kill the running jobs. However, this is a good way of making sure that you don't forget about some jobs that are running.

Background Jobs and STDIN

Since a job that is running in the background does not have access to STDIN, the process will suspend (or pause) itself if the program tries to read input. The next time you get a shell prompt back (and sometimes before then) you will get notification that the background process is requesting input. In most cases, the program will send something to STDOUT with a prompt of some sort. The user will be notified once they get another shell prompt that a background process is awaiting input.

CHAPTER
5

- Kill and Signals

- Finding Other Users on the System

- Communicating with Other Users

The Multi-user
System

S ince Linux allows your hardware to handle many different people using
the CPU at once, there must be some way to communicate between two
users. And how does Linux know which user is running which program?

To illustrate some of what multi-user and time sharing is, I'll introduce the ps
command which is used to display the processes currently running. Think of the
ps as 'process status,' since that is what the command does. First, let's run ps
with no options:

```
> ps
PID TTY STAT   TIME COMMAND
 54 p 2 S      0:00 -tcsh
156 p 2 S      0:00 sh /usr/X11/bin/startx
157 p 2 S      0:00 xinit /usr/X11R6/lib/X11/xinit/xinitrc --
160 p 2 S      0:00 sh /usr/X11R6/lib/X11/xinit/xinitrc
162 p 2 S      0:00 fvwm
165 p 2 S      0:00 /usr/lib/X11/fvwm/GoodStuff 10 4 /home/mark/.fvwmrc 0 8
166 p 2 S      0:00 /usr/lib/X11/fvwm/FvwmPager 12 4 /home/mark/.fvwmrc 0 8 0
170 pp0 S      0:00 -csh
172 pp1 S      0:00 -csh
183 pp2 S      0:00 -csh
221 pp0 R      0:00 ps
```

This looks like a lot of information, but it's easy to break down. The column all the way on the left shows the Process' ID. Each process gets a unique PID to separate it from other processes.

The next column shows the TTY device that the process was run from. The p 2 means that I'm using the second virtual console (the virtual consoles range from 1–8 on most Linux systems). The pp0, pp1, and pp2 refer to shells started while using the X-Window System, called xterm. Each xterm uses a ttyp device, starting at 0 and going up from there. The ttyp devices are also known as ptys, or pseudo-ttys. This is for users who are not sitting directly at the console, or logged in via a serial port. Any user who logs in via TCP/IP or starts an xterm window is connecting via a pty.

The third column shows the status of the process. The s means that the process is sleeping until the CPU can get to it. This is normal, since only one process can run on the CPU at a time, and that process happens to be the ps command itself. There is also W, meaning that the process is not in physical memory at all, but is swapped out to the virtual memory on the hard drive. You'll typically see SW in this case, and you can think of it as 'swapped out.' If you see a T, it means the process is stopped or is being traced. This is the state of a process if you pause it (using CTRL-Z) and do not put it in the background or restart it in the foreground.

The last column shows the name and options given to the process. There are four shells, one ps, and some other processes associated with the X-Window System.

This may look like a lot of processes, but that's not all of the processes that are running. By default, the ps command only shows you the process your userid started. So in my case there are eleven processes that I started. Now let's see everything that is running on the system, by giving the -aux options to ps. The a option means to show all processes of all users. The u means to give the report in user format, giving the user name and start time of the process. The x means to show processes which may not have terminals attached to them.

That looks like a lot more processes, and most of them are owned by the root user. This output gives much more detail about the processes that are running. The first column gives the username of the owner of the process. Then comes the PID. Note that PID 1 is the init process. We'll get to this important process later on.

The next two columns show the percentage of CPU and memory used by the process. This is a fast way of finding processes that take up too much memory or are CPU hogs.

The next two columns show the amount of memory actually used by the process in kilobytes, followed by the total memory usage of the process. The second number is usually larger, since it does not take into account shared memory. For example, the xterm processes are able to share common routines between them.

```
> ps -aux
USER       PID %CPU %MEM SIZE  RSS TTY  STAT START   TIME COMMAND
mark        54  0.0  3.4  350  520 p 2  S    16:06   0:00 -tcsh
mark       156  0.0  2.6  340  396 p 2  S    16:51   0:00 sh /usr/X11/bin/start
mark       157  0.0  2.0   60  308 p 2  S    16:51   0:00 xinit /usr/X11R6/lib/
mark       160  0.0  2.6  341  396 p 2  S    16:51   0:00 sh /usr/X11R6/lib/X11
mark       162  0.0  4.2  193  636 p 2  S    16:51   0:00 fvwm
mark       165  0.0  3.8  101  580 p 2  S    16:51   0:00 /usr/lib/X11/fvwm/Goo
mark       166  0.0  2.8   93  428 p 2  S    16:51   0:00 /usr/lib/X11/fvwm/Fvw
mark       170  0.0  3.2  357  484 pp0  S    16:51   0:00 -csh
mark       172  0.0  3.0  364  460 pp1  S    16:51   0:00 -csh
mark       183  0.0  3.1  355  468 pp2  S    16:55   0:00 -csh
mark       236  0.0  2.1  153  324 pp0  R    18:28   0:00 ps -aux
root         1  0.0  1.5   44  228 con  S    16:06   0:00 init
root         6  0.0  1.0   24  156 con  S    16:06   0:00 bdflush (daemon)
root         7  0.0  1.0   24  160 con  S    16:06   0:00 update (bdflush)
root        25  0.0  1.5   56  228 con  S    16:06   0:00 /usr/sbin/crond -l10
root        42  0.0  1.8   73  280 con  S    16:06   0:00 /usr/sbin/syslogd
root        44  0.0  1.5   40  236 con  S    16:06   0:00 /usr/sbin/klogd
root        46  0.0  1.7   72  268 con  S    16:06   0:00 /usr/sbin/inetd
root        48  0.0  1.5   64  232 con  S    16:06   0:00 /usr/sbin/lpd
root        55  0.0  1.4   41  220 p 3  S    16:06   0:00 /sbin/agetty 38400 tt
root        56  0.0  1.4   41  220 p 4  S    16:06   0:00 /sbin/agetty 38400 tt
root        57  0.0  1.4   41  220 p 5  S    16:06   0:00 /sbin/agetty 38400 tt
root        58  0.0  1.4   41  220 p 6  S    16:06   0:00 /sbin/agetty 38400 tt
root       158  0.6 12.0 2084 1804 con  S    16:51   0:35 X :0
root       169  0.0  6.9  252 1044 p 2  S    16:51   0:00 xterm -geometry 80x64
root       171  0.0  6.5  220  984 p 2  S    16:51   0:00 xterm
root       182  0.0  6.6  224 1000 p 2  S    16:55   0:00 xterm
root       187  0.0  3.4  393  524 pp2  S    16:56   0:00 sh
root       190  0.0  6.8  157 1032 pp2  S    16:56   0:03 xedit chap1
root       203  0.0  1.4   41  220 p 1  S    17:46   0:00 /sbin/agetty 38400 tt
>
```

Next come the controlling terminal and the process status. The processes that have a terminal of con refer to the console, and not any one tty. Again the only process that has a status of R is the ps -aux process. After this is the time the process was started followed by the amount of CPU time used by the program, in hours and minutes. The xedit program has taken up three minutes of CPU time, while the xterms have taken less than a minute of CPU time each. CPU time should not be confused with real time used, since the real time of these processes can be found by taking the current time and subtracting the start time from that. The CPU time asks if the CPU gave 100% of its processing time to this process, how much time would it take to get to the point where it is now? Since most processes don't use the CPU much, this time is usually quite minimal.

If I have a process that seems to be taking up too much CPU time, I can use the renice command to change the priority of the command. By lowering the priority, the system does not give as much CPU time to that process, and other processes get a larger slice of CPU time.

Kill and Signals

There is a kill command, used to send a signal to a running process. This signal is a way to alter or stop an already running process. For example, you can kill a process by sending the SIGKILL signal to the process. This tells the process, "I really don't care what you're doing, quit NOW".

The SIGHUP signal in some cases tells the process to reread its configuration files without actually stopping the program. This is great for testing various kinds of configuration files without having to stop and restart the process. For example, if a configuration for your e-mail server were to change, you could send it a SIGHUP to make it reread its files. In this situation, the e-mail server would not have to be stopped.

Linux supports about thirty different signals, such as SIGPWR, which tells the process if power is lost to the machine. In this case, it would be a signal from, say an uninterruptable power supply that it lost power and the system should shut down soon before the batteries die. It is up to the process to interpret these signals, usually in a manner consistent with the type of signal it receives. There are also two user-defined signals which allow the process to define what it wants to do once it receives that particular signal. For example, it could dump debugging information to a file so that you can examine it while the process is still running. The man-pages for many programs will tell you what signals it recognizes and what it does when receiving these signals.

The most important signal is the SIGKILL, since all processes accept this signal. This is comparable to having a process in DOS that is running and using CTRL-C to stop the program.

The signals that Linux knows about are listed in `/usr/include/asm/signal.h`. Also listed is a number next to the signal:

```
#define SIGHUP        1
#define SIGINT        2
#define SIGQUIT       3
#define SIGILL        4
#define SIGTRAP       5
#define SIGABRT       6
#define SIGIOT        6
#define SIGBUS        7
#define SIGFPE        8
#define SIGKILL       9
```

These signals can also be used as an option to the `kill` command. These two commands do the exact same thing:

```
kill -KILL 153
kill -9 153
```

Since SIGKILL has an entry of 9, it is usually better to use the name (-KILL) instead of the number (-9) for the command, since other systems may not have the same signal list as your Linux machine. Also, the names are a bit easier to remember.

Finding Other Users on the System

The above process listing isn't too helpful in telling me who else is logged in, since I would have to find all instances of shells and relate that to a userid. There is a better way to find out which users are currently logged in by using the `w` or `who` command. The two commands give the same basic information, but in different formats. The `w` command lists who is logged in, when they logged in, how idle they are, and the command they are currently running. The `who` command lists who is logged on, and where they logged in from.

```
> w
11:04am  up 2 days, 24 min,  1 user,  load average: 0.00, 0.00, 0.00
User    tty      from            login@  idle  JCPU   PCPU  what
mark    tty1                     10:41am                    w
```

Looking at this example, it is easy to determine who is logged on to the machine. I'm the only one logged in as an interactive user. There may be FTP connections or other kinds of connections going on behind the scenes, but there is only one person who has an interactive shell running. The above information tells a lot about the system in general. The current time and time since the machine was last started is displayed on the first line, along with the number of users logged in, and the load average for right now, five minutes ago, and fifteen minutes ago. The load average shows a number relating to how heavily the CPU is being used. The more programs running, the higher the load average.

This same information can be shown without the user listing by using the `uptime` command:

```
> uptime
11:04am up 2 days, 24 min, 1 user, load average: 0.00, 0.00, 0.00
>
```

The `who` command lists merely which users are logged in and where they logged in from.

```
> who
mark ttyp1 Apr 26 10:41 (152.127.1.95)
>
```

Here you can see that I am logged in on ttyp1 (a virtual terminal), the time and date when I logged in, and where I logged in from; in this case, an external TCP/IP machine.

Communicating with Other Users

When you see that two users are logged in, for example the users mark and gonzo, these two users can communicate with each other through various means. The most common ways to do this are: write, talk, and mail.

Write

The write command allows you to write a message directly to another user's screen. When you write to another user, the other user receives a message informing them that another user is writing to their terminal.

```
> write gonzo

blah

<Hit CTRL-D here>

>
```

Gonzo sees:

```
Message from mfk@linux on ttyp0 at 11:39 ...
blah
EOF
```

The EOF means 'End Of File', signalling that mark has ended the write command. While this command is useful, it can often be annoying when not used
properly. The user receiving the message will have the text appear on his screen.
If the user was editing a file or reading mail, this will make the screen look gar-
bled. Some programs, like vi or some of the shells, allow you to use the CTRL-R
or CTRL-L keys to redraw the screen if this happens.

If you do not wish to receive messages, you can use the mesg command to allow
or deny write commands to your screen. mesg y will allow write commands,
while mesg n denies write commands. If a user tries to write to your screen
while messages are disabled for you, the user will see this:

```
> write gonzo
write: gonzo has messages disabled on ttyp1
>
```

The talk command is more of a two-way communication than write is. Talk
splits the screen in half. The top half is for the person locally, and the bottom half
is for the person you're talking to.

Talk is a bit nicer to the user that you want to talk to. The user receives a talk request instead of the actual message you want to convey. Essentially, write alerts
the user that you want to talk to him and gives the message while talk merely
alerts the user that you want to talk to him.

To initate a talk session, you type talk followed by the user you want to talk to:

```
> talk gonzo
```

At this point, your screen will clear and split in two. The very top line will give
status information about the talk request to the remote user. You can get messages such as, "ringing remote party" or, "remote party not logged on" or, "connection established." If the other user is logged on, they will see something like
this:

```
Message from Talk_Daemon@trippy at 11:54 ...
talk: connection requested by mark@trippy.wizvax.net.
talk: respond with: talk mark@trippy.wizvax.net
```

At this point, the other user can type in talk mark or talk mark@trippy.wiz-
vax.net and the talk session is established. The two users can begin typing
messages.

The other user can ignore the messages, and the caller will probably give up after a few minutes. The talk requests will continue until the user initiating the talk request leaves the talk program. Talk requests will usually occur every fifteen to twenty seconds.

The callee can also deny talk requests in the same manner as denying write requests using the `mesg` command.

Netiquette

There are nice ways and not so nice ways of using the write and talk features of Linux. Depending on the individual, you may want to use talk more frequently than write.

Here's how I handle communication with users on the same system. If the user is logged in and using the shell, fire up a talk request. If the user doesn't respond in a minute or so, cancel the talk request. If the user is logged in and using a program, send a write message requesting a talk session, then leave yourself at a shell prompt. At the other user's convenience, he or she can initiate a talk session and the two of you can talk.

Mail

If the other user isn't logged on, there are ways to communicate. E-mail is fast becoming the most popular method of communication over the Internet. The advantages are easy to see:

1. Easy to use

2. Allows for communication between any two (or more) users on the Internet

3. A vast majority of the Internet machines support it.

The e-mail system that the Internet uses is called SMTP for Simple Mail Transport Protocol, defined in RFC 871. The RFC specifies how e-mail gets passed from one machine to another, either by going directly from Machine A to Machine D, or by routing through Machine B and Machine C along the way. Fortunately, much of the work of configuring mail is trivial for a small Linux site. For now, I'll describe how two users on the same system can communicate to each other using the mail program.

Mail is stored on each system in a common location. For Linux, this is usually the `/var/spool/mail/` directory. Each user has a mailbox which is their username. For example, for the mark account, there exists a `/var/spool/mail/mark` file. It's owned by each user so that only that user can open and read the file, providing security against anyone (except root or anyone who has root powers) from reading the file.

Let's look at the case where the gonzo user wants to send the mark user an e-mail note. If gonzo wants to know when mark is having lunch, he can

1. Start the mail program, specifying mark as the user to send the mail to

2. Write the e-mail message

3. End the mail program and let mail send the message to mark.

Let's renew these steps in detail:

1. From the shell prompt, gonzo would type `mail mark`. If there were more people gonzo wanted to send the message to, they can be specified on the same line like this:

   `mail mark bren neal`

2. The default mail reader is slightly harder to use than other, friendlier mail programs, but since most Linux installations have mail, along with most UNIX sites in general, it is important to know. The default mail program is also the fastest in terms of just sending a quick note, as opposed to diving through menus and remembering key sequences.

   The first thing mail will ask you for is a subject, which will be one of the first things that the other users will see upon reading the e-mail message. This should be under forty characters and sum up the purpose of the message; for example, "Lunch at noon?"

   Gonzo can now start typing his note just as if he were writing a file. The only things to remember are to hit the enter key at the end of each line, and that a line cannot start with a tilde (~). Using a tilde at the beginning of a line tells mail that you want to do something special. Here's a list of some of the ~ commands and what they do:

   ~r<file> - read in the contents of the file

   ~v - activate the editor

   ~! - activate a shell

   ~p - print out the message as it reads so far

   ~s<string> - change the subject of the mail message to <string>

   If you choose to abort sending the message, you can hit CTRL-C twice and you'll be returned to the shell prompt.

3. Once the message is done, you get on a line by itself and hit CTRL-D. This tells the mail program that the message is complete and you are ready to send it. The last thing that mail will ask you for is CC: or carbon copies.

These may be people not directly affected by the message, but may be interested in the contents, such as asking the gang at work to a long lunch, then CC: to the boss to make sure it's okay.

Here's how gonzo's mail session looks:

```
> mail mark bren neal
Subject: Lunch at noon?
Hey guys,
How about we have lunch at the new restaurant, the Linux Lun-
cheon? I hear they have great prices. Here's a copy of their
menu:
~rlinuxluncheon
"linuxluncheon" 9/149
Cc: daboss
>
```

Now, whether or not any of the users are logged in, they'll have that mail waiting for them the next time they log on. If they are logged on, a message will appear on their screen telling them that another user has sent them mail. At any rate, the next time bren, mark, neal, or daboss logs in, they'll get a message saying

```
You have new mail.
```

At this point, the user can check his or her e-mail and read the message. To do this, just type `mail`. If you have mail, you'll see something similar to this:

```
> mail
Mail version 5.5 6/1/90. Type ? for help.
"/var/spool/mail/mark": 1 message 1 new
>N 1 gonzo       Mon May 1 17:55 26/608 "Lunch at noon?"
&
```

The ampersand (&) is the prompt while you're in the mail program. Note how the mail program handles two different functions at once—displaying and sending mail.

You can see in our example that there is one message in mark's system mailbox, which is located in the file `/var/spool/mail/mark`. There is also a listing of the mail messages, who they're from, when each message was received, the length of the message in lines/characters, and the subject of the message. The two characters all the way to the left of the message tell you the status of the message.

The > tells you that that message is the next in line to be read. If you hit the enter key, the message would be displayed. The N tells you that the message is new and unread. There are also statuses of O for old, but unread, and blank, meaning it has been read and is old. New in this case refers to when you last used the mail program.

CHAPTER
6

- Editing Files (vi, joe, emacs)

- How to Use vi

- Commands

- File Management (File Manager and DOS Commands)

- Format and MKFS

- Man/Whatis and Help

- Whatis Database

User Programs

The best way of learning something new (in this case, an entire operating system) is to compare it to something you already know and note the differences. This chapter will cover some of the programs that are standard on a Windows and DOS machine and show you what the Linux counterparts are and how they work.

Editing Files (vi, joe, emacs)

Until the BSD release of UNIX, the default editor (called ed) was a line-by-line editor, much like edlin was in DOS releases before 5.0. The BSD release introduced the vi program for visual editor. It is a full screen editor, but it retains much of the functionality of the earlier line-based editors. The advantages to this are that vi was able to be used very quickly by users of the previous system. In addition, many of the macros and commands used in ed could still be used in vi.

As a result of this setup, the vi editor has two modes: command and editing. The command mode is where macros or other commands could be entered, such as doing a global search and replace, find, or just moving the cursor to a different part of the screen. The editing mode allowed you to enter text much like you would with any other text editor. Since the technology behind vi is at least ten years old, this seems like an inefficient method of editing a file. But, once you learn how vi works, it's relatively easy to use and is quite powerful for editing small files. Just as edit and notepad are on just about every DOS and Windows setup, vi will be in most UNIX installations.

How to Use vi

To edit a file, use the command `vi <filename>` where `<filename>` is the file you want to edit. Once the file is loaded, you'll see the first page of the screen displayed, and you'll be in command mode allowing you to move around the file. To add new text to the file, you'll have to switch into edit mode.

Edit Mode

You enter characters and they get echoed to the screen. This includes most control characters. Note that by default, vi won't do word wrapping or other special formatting for you, so be sure to hit enter at the end of each line. There are two main ways to enter edit mode from command mode. Pressing a will append text to the right of where the cursor currently is. Pressing i will insert characters to the left of the cursor. Once you're in edit mode, you can begin typing text in. Be sure to hit the return key at the end of the line. To switch back to command mode from edit mode, hit the ESC key.

Command Mode

The vi editor has two command sections with one of the sections relating to ed commands. These ed commands start with a colon (:). Other commands, mostly involving moving the cursor or changing modes, do not have a colon (:).

x	- Delete the character under the cursor
dd	- Delete the entire line
^f	- Go forward one screen
^u or ^b	- Go back one screen
h	- Move the cursor back one character
j	- Move the cursor down one line
k	- Move the cursor up one line
l	- Move the cursor left one character
/<text>	- Search forward for <text>
ZZ	- Save the file and quit
J	- Combine this line with the next line, to make one line
^L	- Redraw the screen
o	- Go to the first column
H	- Go to the beginning of the document

Most of the above commands can be prefaced with a number to allow you to perform the command that number of times. For example, you could delete ten lines by typing:

10dd

The other commands include the search and replace functions in the ed editor:

```
:q!                     -quit without saving
:r<filename>            -read in <filename> and insert it at the current cursor
                         location
:s/<txta>/<txtb>/g  -replace <txta> with <txtb> in the current line
:w<filename>            -write what is in the editor to <filename>
```

One interesting feature of the replace text feature (:s) is that you can select a list of lines to replace the text in by putting it before the s. You put the first line, followed by a comma, followed by the last line you want. You can replace the last line number (if you don't know it) with a $. For example, the command

```
:1,$s/ />/g
```

will replace all spaces with a > character in all the lines.

You can include other regular expressions in the replacement as well. You can find more about regular expressions in Chapter 7.

joe

The next editor, which is standard on many Linux installations, is the joe editor, which stands for Joe's Own Editor. This may remind you of a program closer to Wordstar or early Borland IDE editors with its range of control keys.

Unlike vi, joe provides more default functions such as default word wrapping, multiple windows, and on-line help.

To start joe, type

```
> joe <filename>
```

where <filename> is the name of the file you wish to edit.

joe doesn't have two modes to it—only the one which combines the editing and command functions. Many of the commands have a prefix of ^K, but not all. Here are some of the more familiar commands used in joe:

^U   - Forward one screen

^V   - Back one screen

^Y   - Delete the entire line

^C   - Quit without saving

^A   - Go to the beginning of the line

^KH   - Display help screen, or close it if there is one already up

^KF   - Find a word (also for replacing)

^KX   - Save file and quit

^KD   - Save file as a specified filename (you'll get asked for it)

^KB   - Define the beginning of a block

^KK   - Define the end of a block

^KM   - Move a predefined block to the current location

^KC   - Copy the block to the current location

^K| - Pipe the text in a block through a program

The disadvantage to joe is that not all UNIX machines have it installed. Most Linux machines may have it installed, since it is included with many distributions.

emacs

To many, the emacs program is more than just an editor, it's a mail reader, news reader, FTP client, and many other components all in one. The downside to emacs is that it's a rather large program: the binary itself being almost two megabytes in size as compared to 136k for joe and about 100k for vi.

The other downside is the complexity of the program itself. It almost makes learning vi look easy. The program relies heavily on an extensive number of control sequences and keys that can give your fingers a workout.

The advantages, however, are impressive. It takes the functionality of vi and raises it a notch by including its own lisp interpreter. This allows even more powerful functions for an editor, such as starting up shells from within an edit window, auto-FTPing a file and editing it, reading USENET news, and even reading your mail—all without leaving the editor. For emacs advocates, emacs isn't just an editor—it's a way of life.

To start emacs type

```
> emacs <filename>
```

where `<filename>` is the name of the file that you would like to edit.

Note the following movement commands:

^v	Page down
Esc v	Page up
^f	Forward one character
^b	Back one character
^n	Down one line
^p	Up one line
^k	Delete to end of line
^a	Go to beginning of line
^e	Go to end of line

Note the following search commands:

`^s`	Search forward (prompts for criteria)
`^r`	Search reverse (prompts for criteria)
`Esc-x replace-string`	Search and replace all (prompts for string and re-placement)
`Esc-X query-replace`	Search and replace (asks to replace each occurrence of the string)

The following is a list of buffer commands:

`^x^o`	Switch between buffers
`^x^k`	Kill buffer (prompts to save file)
`^x^s`	Save buffer
`^x^w`	Save buffer as (prompts for filename)

This is a list of block commands (current cursor position defines end of block):

`^<space-bar>`	Sets beginning of block
`^w`	Cut from point to beginning of block and insert into kill ring
`Alt-W`	Copy from point to beginning of block into kill ring
`^y`	Yank first entry of kill ring and insert at current point
`^k`	Cuts from point to end of line to kill ring

This is a list of shell commands:

`Esc-x shell`	Starts a shell in the emacs session
`Esc-x man`	Bring up a man-page (prompts for a command)
`Esc-x shell-command`	Run any shell command directly from the minibuffer

Type and More/Less

The command for viewing the contents of a file one page at a time doesn't quite exist in Windows, unless you load the file into something like notepad and scroll through it. DOS has the `type` and `more` commands, usually put together in the form

```
type <file> | more
```

since `more <file>` gives you an error under DOS. In order to use `more` under DOS it requires using

```
more < type
```

Not to worry, however, since Linux supports the `more <file>` command line, and improved upon viewing a file a screenful at a time by including such things as scrolling backwards in the file, editing the file as you view it, and showing how much of the file you've viewed so far. These features are helpful for very large files.

There are two commands in Linux that are the equivalent of `more` in DOS. The first is `more`, which is the default program. The other is called `less` which means 'less is more'. Not only are many UNIX programmers good, they have a sense of existentialism—or twisted humor. You decide.

The less program provides extra functionality over the regular more program such as displaying the current line and the total number of lines in the file and some extra searching capabilities.

To start viewing a file using more or less, the command is the same:

```
less <filename>
```

Commands

There are a few useful commands that you can use from within more (or less):

`(space)`	- Move to the next page
`(return)`	- Move to the next line
`h`	- On-line help
`b`	- Move back one page
`:n`	- If viewing multiple files (such as `more *.txt`) go to the next file
`v`	- Begin editing the file at the current line
`=`	- Display current line number
`q`	- Quit
`/<text>`	- Search forward for <text>

Many of these commands can be prefaced with a number to run that command some number of times. The command

```
5b
```

will bring you back five pages.

File Management (File Manager and DOS Commands)

The ZIP format of file compression in DOS has its counterpart in the Linux world through the use of two programs: gzip and tar.

The tar program was originally used for backing up files to a tape backup unit, but is now being used to combine all sorts of files together for distribution throughout the Internet. In conjunction with the gzip program, this provides a means of compressing large groups of files and preserving things like file owner-ship, permissions, and file links. These are not parts of the standard ZIP format since DOS has no real sense of these things.

The gzip (for gnu zip) program will compress a single file using the ZIP format. In some cases, the file can be uncompressed by a program such as PKUNZIP in the DOS world, WinUnzip from Windows, or gunzip for DOS.

To compress a file, just type `gzip <filename>`. To fine-tune the compression, you can use the `-#` option, where # is a number between 1 and 9. A compression number of 1 has the least compression but is the fastest to compress, while 9 has the highest compression but takes longer to compress with a default number of 6. You can also use the `-v` option to print verbose information of compression, mostly giving the compression ratio. English text files will see the best compres-sion, with a ratio of between 60% and 70%, and executable files getting slightly less all the way down to precompressed files such as GIF or JPEG images, which have very little if any compression.

When you compress the file, the original file gets erased after the compressed file is created. The filename of the compressed file is the same as the original name, with a `.gz` at the end. If I compressed a file called `text.txt`, the compressed file would be called `text.txt.gz`.

To uncompress a file, you can use `gunzip <file>` or `gzip -d <file>`.

Along the same line, most other commands for modifying files are done at the command line, unlike the point-and-click that is available for Windows-based operating systems. For example, copying files in Windows is as simple as drag-ging the file and dropping it on the directory you want to copy it to. Linux, on the other hand is much more like DOS where you have to list the directory you're copying from and where you're copying it to. To copy a file from my home directory to the home directory of gonzo I would use a command like this:

```
> cp /home/mark/foo.txt /home/gonzo/files/
```

(Assuming, of course, that gonzo had set his permissions such that I could put files in his directory, which is a possible security risk in itself.)

Other commands include the following:

`chmod <permissions> <file>` - Changing permissions on a file

`chown <user.group> <file>` - Change owner of a file

`rm <file>` - Delete a file

```
cp <source> <destination>   - Copy a file
mv <source> <destination>   - Move a file
```

For compatability with MS-DOS, not only is mounting an MS-DOS FAT drive supported, but you can use a package called mtools to read and write to floppy drives and hard disk drives as well.

Mounting an MS-DOS disk requires that you have FAT support listed in your kernel. This is an option you'll get when the kernel gets recompiled. Once that is done, determine which DOS drive you want to mount based on which partition it is. In most cases, the C: drive is the first partition on the first disk drive, so a command like this (as root):

```
# mount -t msdos /dev/hda1 /mnt
```

will mount the msdos disk on the /mnt directory. If you have an SCSI-based system, the command is

```
# mount -t msdos /dev/sda1 /mnt
```

Be sure that the /mnt directory exists.

Once that is complete, you can then work on the MS-DOS drive just like a Linux partition.

The mtools package allows you to change files on an MS-DOS drive without needing support in the kernel or mounting the drive. It contains a number of utilities to perform functions like this:

mformat   - Format a drive in FAT format

mcopy   - Copy a file to/from a FAT drive

mdel   - Delete a file

mdir   - Get a directory

These are the most common functions. There are others including labels, change directory, creating and removing directories, and more. Check the mtools manpage to find out more about how it works.

Format and MKFS

Creating a new partition under MSDOS was as easy as typing

```
C:\> FORMAT D:
```

Unfortunately, under Linux, this isn't quite so easy. But it's close. In order to have added functionality like long filenames, file ownership and permissions, and extensions for future functionality, Linux has three different native filesystems that you can use. There's the Linux/Minix format, based on the original Minix format. This format has very limited extended filename support, ownership and permissions, and is not widely used now due to the advantages that the other filesystems have.

The second format is the xiafs for XIA format. This format was developed as an alternative to the Minix filesystem, adding 255 character filenames. This isn't used much either, since the third filesystem we'll look at (EXT2) is the most popular and the most widely used filesystem.

So on to the EXT2. for Second Extended Filesystem. The first Extended Filesystem was similar to XIA, and the second version of the EXT filesystem allowed for future enhancements, and is a bit faster at finding files.

There is one thing to note while making EXT2 partitions. Making a partition that is 100M big will appear to have only 95M free, for an apparent loss of about 5%. Why is this? There are two reasons. First, EXT2 partitions don't suffer from fragmentation that FAT partitions have. FAT partitions need to be frequently defragmented by a program like DEFRAG or SPEEDISK to keep the partition running at peak efficiency. EXT2 partitions have algorithms built in to keep the files as defragmented as possible, and doing this requires some minimum amount of space set aside for the filesystem code to keep files defragmented.

The second reason is that only the root user is allowed to write to this space, which is good for emergency situations.

To create a filesystem, type

```
> mke2fs -c <partition> [<blocks>]
```

where `<partition>` is the partition you want to create. The `-c` option tells `mke2fs` to do a quick check for any kind of bad blocks while it creates the partition. An option is the number of blocks to make the filesystem. Some older versions of mke2fs require you to enter the size of the partition you are making. Newer versions (at least after version 0.5c) know how big the partition is and you may not have to enter it in. You can specify other options, such as `-m <percent>` which tells mke2fs to reserve `<percent>` for the super user. The default is 5%. It's a good idea not to modify this value, since making the number low will severely degrade the performance of the filesystem. Making the number too high will not greatly increase the speed of the partition, resulting in a possible loss of space.

Once the partition is created, you can use it immediately by mounting it (as root) and moving files there or however you intend to use the partition.

Man/Whatis and Help

The DOS help program after DOS 5.0 shows some of the same concepts used in the Linux man program. Both give you a listing of the program, how it works, possibly some sample setups, and provide links to similar programs that you may be interested in seeing help for. But this is where the similarity ends. The Linux man program doesn't have any kind of hyperlinks, forcing you to jump around manually finding programs. But you are allowed (encouraged) to add your own new man-pages as you install new programs. The DOS help program is limited to programs related to DOS only, but Linux man provides help on most of the programs you already installed, plus you can add new man pages and have them available immediately.

There are a few locations where man-pages can be kept, but under that, the directory structure is the same:

`/usr/man`

`/var/man`

`/usr/local/man`

Under each of these directories, there are about twenty other directories split into two major groups:

man[1–9]—These man pages are in a raw format called nroff, which is a text formatting program. These are the sources of the manual pages.

cat[1–9]—These are the man pages already compiled by nroff in a format which gets displayed to the user very quickly, since it is already compiled.

The advantage to having man pages in nroff format is that it allows for things like highlighting and underlining, along with support for automatically formatting text.

When the man program looks for a man-page, it follows the set of directories listed in the MANPATH environment variable. My MANPATH reads

```
MANPATH=/usr/local/man:/usr/man/preformat:/usr/man:
         /usr/X11/man:/usr/openwin/man
```

Meaning that it first looks under the `/usr/local/man` directory, then under the `/usr/man/preformat` directory, and so on. First, man looks in the `cat` directories to see if it can find the man-page, then goes to the `man` directories and checks there. If the man program finds a file in the `cat` directory that matches the request you gave, it displays that to the user. Otherwise, the man program searches the man directories to see if there is an `nroff source` file.

Once man has gone through all the paths and determined that a given program has no manual pages, it comes back with:

```
> man noprog
No manual entry for noprog
>
```

Whatis Database

One file that is associated with the man program is the `whatis` file, located in `/usr/man`. This file contains the first line of each manual page. This line looks something like this:

```
ls, dir, vdir (1)
```

This lists contents of directories.

The important part of this line is the first part, which has the names of the commands, the second part has the section number in it, and the part to the right, has a description of what the program does. This database can be searched for complete words, or for substrings.

Apropos searches the whatis database based on incomplete strings. That is, if you're looking for an apropos listing on the word man, you'll get a whole list of programs that has the three letters 'man' in its description. Words such as command, man, manual, manage, demand, and so on will be found. This will make the list of commands you get back rather large. The command `apropos man` returned over 100 commands that have the three letters 'man' in it.

The whatis program searches for complete words. Only entries that contain the three letter word 'man' surrounded by spaces gets listed. This can make the list of commands you get very short. The command `whatis man` returned three commands.

BC

Need a calculator? You have a rather powerful one sitting right in front of you, so why not use it? The bc program provides you with an interactive calculator that is also programmable. In fact, the man-pages include the code for a simple checkbook balancing program.

Simple arithmetic statements can be entered just as you would write them:

```
5+3 <enter>
8
```

For division or answers that require precision, you can use the `scale` command to set how many digits past the decimal point you want. Remember that this is truncating instead of rounding:

```
scale=3 <enter>
1/6 <enter>
.166
```

You can also switch to different bases using the `ibase` command. The different kinds of bases you can use range from 2 (binary) through 16 (hexidecimal). This sets the input base. The `obase` command sets the base of the output. This allows for easy conversion among bases such as, hex to decimal. The default `ibase` and `obase` is 10 (decimal).

This is how the numbers got converted from hex to decimal, then to binary.

```
ibase=16 <enter>
```

```
FF <enter>
```

```
255
```

```
obase=2 <enter>
```

```
FF <enter>
```

```
11111111
```

Running bc with the `-l` option will add in some math libraries, so that you can compute sines, cosines, logarithms, and a few other functions. Nothing like knowing what pi is to twenty decimal places:

```
>bc -l
```

```
4*a(1) <enter>
```

```
3.14159265358979323844
```

The bc man pages can tell more about bc.

File

The `file` command can usually tell you what kind of data is in a particular file. It does this by looking in the `/usr/lib/magic` file for information about different kinds of applications, executables, and so on. It then looks at the file you're requesting information on and looks it up.

The idea is that each file has a few characters in the front of the file that separates it from other kinds of files. For example, `postscript` files which are used for some forms of laser printers, begin with the characters `%!`. If a file starts with these two characters, then it is likely that this file is a `postscript` file. The `/usr/lib/magic` (it may also be in `/etc/magic`) has information on all kinds of files, from music files to executables, even executables for other operating systems, such as NetBSD or BSDI.

In some cases, a file can tell you information about the file:

```
> file fall.gif
fall.gif: GIF image—version 87a 46 x 45, 2 colors
>
> file linux-1.3.59.tar.gz
linux-1.3.59.tar.gz: gzip compressed data—deflate method , last
modified: Tue Jan 23 17:36:59 1996 , max compression os: Unix
>
```

CHAPTER 7

- GREP—General Regular Expression Parser
- Find
- PWD
- Kill
- Cron
- joe
- Diff

Extra Programs

There are a number of standard utilities that come with Linux that have no standard counterparts in DOS, Windows, or OS/2. Some of these utilities have been ported to these operating systems, and many are GNU products.

GREP—General Regular Expression Parser

A regular expression is a way of doing pattern matching to match a piece of text within a given file. This regular expression is used in many programs from GNU, even the bash shell. The program used to match a piece of text within a given file or set of files is called grep. You may recognize grep from some Borland compilers in DOS.

The way a regular expression works is that the expression (often called a regexp) is matched from beginning to end. As a piece of text is searched, if it matches the current point in the regexp, it advances a pointer through both the regexp and the text to be searched. If grep reaches the end of the regexp, it knows that that regexp exists in the searched text and returns it.

A regexp is much more advanced than just a simple search for a piece of text. Special characters are used to group sections of characters together, or represent special cases for matching a character. Some of the expressions that can be used in grep are listed here:

.   - Any character

[(chars)]   - Any of the characters inside the parenthesis

[x–y]   - Any number including and between x and y

[A–Z]   - Any capital letter [a–z] or lowercase letter

^	- If at the beginning of a regular expression, it indicates that this regular expression should be found at the beginning of the line
$	- At the end of a regular expression, it indicates that the preceding text is at the end of a line
*	- The preceding character can be repeated at least 0 times (i.e., it may not occur in the text, or once, or more
?	- The preceding character is matched at most once (i.e., either it occurs once, or it doesn't)
+	- The preceding character occurs one or more times; if the character isn't at that position, it's not a match
\	- An escape character that allows you to search for characters like * and [within a file.

So, a regular expression of

```
^Mark.*
```

would match any lines that start with the letters "Mark" while

```
^M.rk
```

could match

```
Mark
```

```
Mork
```

```
Merk
```

```
Mbck
```

```
M9ck
```

And a regular expression of

```
^M[aeiouAEIOU]rk
```

would match

```
Mark
```

```
MArk
```

```
Merk
```

```
MErk
```

but not

```
Mbrk
```

Find

Since files can be literally scattered all over the filesystem, there has to be a way of finding a file and then optionally performing some action on that file (like remove it, or just tell you where the file is located). The `find` command allows you to search the filesystem for various files. The `find` command allows you to search based on regular expressions, much like the `grep` command.

The generic format of the find command is

```
find -name <file>
```

Where `<file>` is the filename (or regexp) that you are looking for. But name is not the only locator for files.

By default, the `find` command starts at the current working directory and begins searching directories underneath that directory. Some versions of `find` require a starting directory, so you may have to use a period, which indicates the current directory. To find the file using another start directory, you can include a directory right after the `find` command. For example, to search all of the mounted directories, you can use the command

```
> find / -name "search_file"
/home/mark/search_file
>
```

Using other tools, you can have the `find` command run a program on each of the files that it finds. For example, you could have temporary files deleted. One common way of reclaiming disk space is deleting object files (.o) from a program you compiled and ran. Another useful function is to use grep on more than one directory. It allows you to find a string of text when you don't know the file or the directory.

To do this you use the `-exec` option. Anything after the `-exec` and up until a semicolon (;) gets executed each time `find` finds a file. For cases where you need to know the name of the file, you use the {}. For example, if you want to remove all the `.o` files that are in the directory `/usr/src` or underneath it, you can run this:

```
> find /usr/src -name "*.o" -exec "rm {}" \;
>
```

Many shells use ; as a special character to separate multiple commands on one line, so we have to make the shell ignore it by using the \ character. Also, if there were not any quotes around the `rm` command, you'd have to also escape the { and the } using the \ character.

Also note that there was no output of the files that match the `*.o`. If you include the `-print` option, it will print the files as they get matched. This is a good way of making sure that the files get deleted.

Another option, to find a string in some text is a command similar to

```
> find /usr/src -name "*.h" -exec grep some_text \{\} \;
>
```

This will only tell you if the string exists in some of the text. The problem is that grep has no commands for telling you which file it found the text in. Fortunately, find can tell you what file it's looking through at the current moment with the -ls option. So the command

```
> find /usr/src -name "*.h" -print -exec grep some_text \{\} \;
```

would list all the files that it finds, giving the path for each file it finds.

PWD

The pwd program prints out the present working directory. For shells that don't print out the directory in the prompt, or for shell scripts that need to know the current directory, this is quite helpful. This is similar to the $P entry in the DOS prompt command and the cd command without any options:

```
C> prompt=$p$g
C:\WINDOWS>cd

C:\WINDOWS
C:\WINDOWS>
```

Kill

The kill program can be used to send signals to running programs. A signal is a way of notifying a running program of certain conditions. For example, some programs will reload their configuration files in the case of receiving a signal 1 or SIGHUP. Many programs will end execution when receiving a SIGINT (for interrupt signal), and all running programs will quit if they receive a SIGKILL which is a kill signal.

The way programs work are that one program, known as the parent, executes and then starts other programs, the children. You can see a list of the process IDs (PID) and parent's PID (PPID) using the -l or the -j options to ps:

```
> ps -j
```

PPID	PID	PGID	SID TTY TPGID	STAT	UID	TIME COMMAND
1	101	101	101 p 1 625	S	406	0:00 -tcsh
101	625	625	101 p 1 625	S	406	0:00 sh /usr/X11/bin/startx
625	626	625	101 p 1 625	S	406	0:00 xinit /usr/X11R6/lib/X11/
626	630	630	101 p 1 625	S	406	0:00 sh /usr/X11R6/lib/X11/xin
630	632	630	101 p 1 625	S	406	0:02 fvwm
632	635	630	101 p 1 625	S	406	0:00 /usr/lib/X11/fvwm/GoodStu

```
    632    636    630    101 p 1    625  S      406   0:00 /usr/lib/X11/fvwm/FvwmPag

    632    637    630    101 p 1    625  S      406   0:00 /usr/lib/X11/fvwm/FvwmAud

    640    642    642    642 pp0    956  S      406   0:00 -csh

    643    644    644    644 pp1    948  S      406   0:00 -csh

    644    647    647    644 pp1    948  S      406   0:01 axe chap7

    644    871    871    644 pp1    948  S      406   0:00 sh

    871    948    948    644 pp1    948  S      406   0:06 s3mod -sn icefront.s3m

    642    956    956    642 pp0    956  R      406   0:00 ps -j
> ps -l
F   UID    PID   PPID PRI NI SIZE   RSS WCHAN      STAT TTY   TIME COMMAND
0   406    101      1   1  0 348    456 10fff8     S    p 1   0:00 -tcsh
0   406    625    101   1  0 340    396 10fff8     S    p 1   0:00 sh /usr/X11/b
0   406    626    625   1  0  60    308 11d2ac     S    p 1   0:00 xinit /usr/X1
0   406    630    626   1  0 341    396 10fff8     S    p 1   0:00 sh /usr/X11R6
0   406    632    630   1  0 205    640 1325fd     S    p 1   0:03 fvwm
0   406    635    632   1  0 105    580 1325fd     S    p 1   0:00 /usr/lib/X11/
0   406    636    632   1  0  97    428 1325fd     S    p 1   0:00 /usr/lib/X11/
0   406    637    632   1  0  40    180 117e7e     S    p 1   0:00 /usr/lib/X11/
0   406    642    640   8  0 367    556 10fff8     S    pp0   0:00 -csh
0   406    957    642  20  0 145    300 0          R    pp0   0:00 ps -l
0   406    644    643   1  0 361    500 10fff8     S    pp1   0:00 -csh
0   406    647    644   1  0 339   1120 1325fd     S    pp1   0:01 axe chap7
0   406    871    644   1  0 369    504 10fff8     S    pp1   0:00 sh
0   406    948    871   7  0 421    516 117e7e     S    pp1   0:11 s3mod -sn ice
>
```

You can see the PIDs and PPIDs for the processes in columns three and four. Note that the main shell I'm running (the tcsh) has a PPID of 1, the init process. Then note what processes the tcsh process spawned and what those processes spawned, and so on. To cure the confusion, the parent processes of the shells are xterms that are owned by root.

When the parent process dies or is exited, it often sends a signal to each of its children informing it that it is no longer running. In many cases, this is a SIGHUP. This is why, for example, if you start a big compilation you have to kill the make program itself, as killing the individual C compiler programs won't stop the make, only that one individual compile.

So, now that you know about signals, you ask, "Are there any ways to trap signals?" Yes there are. Two ways in fact. First is the specific case of trapping the SIGHUP signal. Take the case where you start a program that will take a while, perhaps longer than you wish to be logged in. So you start the program and put it in the background. Now the problem exists that when you log out of that shell, the shell will send the background process a SIGHUP and the process terminates before it is completed.

The nohup command allows you to trap and ignore the SIGHUP signal, allowing the process to run to completion. The program is still susceptible to SIGKILL and other signals, so the program can still be killed or interrupted. The syntax for the command is

```
>nohup <command>

>
```

Instead of just running the command, put a nohup in front of it. After this, the program will run just like it normally would with one exception. STDERR and STDOUT are both redirected to either ./nohup.out or $HOME/nohup.out, depending on where nohup can write the file to. Also note that running nohup will not put the program in the background, you still have to do that yourself using either the ^z and bg method, or by adding an & at the end of the line.

The other method, using the /bin/bash shell, is a built-in command called trap. This allows you to trap any signal and run a program upon receiving that signal. One use for this is making secure SUID shell scripts, where you don't want a user to be able to hit CTRL-C or send some other signal to the script. This could cause the script to end and the user to be left with more access than they started with. For example, a shell script that starts with

```
#!/bin/bash

trap exit 2

..

<rest of shell script>

..
```

would cause the script to exit when it recives a SIGINT (signal 2).

One practical example would be to create a login script for a user whose account has been suspended for some reason (the did not log in for six months for example). You could create a shell script like this:

```
#!/bin/bash

trap exit 1 2 3 4 5 6 7 8 9

echo Your account has been temporarily suspended because it
```

```
echo has not been used. Please see the system administrator to re-
activate echo your account. Thank you.
sleep 10
exit
```

This code will run as the user (assuming you set their shell to be this script) and display the above message. In some cases, you can hit the CTRL-C and break out of the script, leaving the user logged in and at a shell prompt. Not very secure, is it? The trap allows you to catch that signal, and then immediately exit from the script. Since the script is the shell, once the script exits in the proper manner, the user is logged out.

Cron

The cron program allows you to schedule jobs to run periodically. Unlike the at command which allows you to start one job at a specific time, the cron entry continues to execute at its periodic interval until you stop it. Advantages are for scheduling backups, weekly scripts to change a data file, or calculating the number of hits your WWW site receives in a day. Cron will even mail you the output of the program that ran.

To set up a cron entry for your user, you have to use the crontab program, which allows you to view, edit, clear, or completely replace the previous entries in the crontab file. Most default Linux installations allow all users to create their own crontab files, while some installations may restrict which users can use crontab. Check the man-pages for cron and crontab for more information about who is allowed use of the system.

Each user has his or her own crontab file stored under /var/spool/cron and is unreadable to all other users except root. Using the crontab -e command, you enter vi or the editor defined in your EDITOR environment variable and you can begin adding entries.

A crontab entry has six fields, separated by at least a space character:

Minute:	Cron has its lowest resolution set to a minute. This can be in the range 0–60 or * for every minute
Hour:	0–24 or * for every hour
Day:	0–31 or * for every day
Month:	0–12 or * for each month
Day of week:	0–6 or * for every day of the week
Command to run:	The command you wish to run. Cron will execute it using: /bin/sh -c <command>.

While the cron entries look simple, they can be combined in ways to make them extremely powerful. For example, to run a program once every four hours, you could use an entry like this:

```
0 */4 * * * script.sh
```

or you can have ranges. To run a command every hour between 11PM and 7AM:

```
0 23-7 * * * script.sh
```

To run the command during the above period, but also at 8AM:

```
0 23-7,8 * * * script.sh
```

Once crontab has completed (when you save the file and exit the editor), it installs the new crontab file and tells cron that a new crontab file has been added. Cron than compiles the new crontab into its own internal format and immediately uses the new entries. Using this internal format, cron can have thousands of entries in its database with little drain on the CPU; the exception being the processes that cron starts up.

Joe

The joe editor stands for Joe's Own Editor and will remind you of an editor like WordStar or Borland's IDE editors. It's simple, fast, has on-line help, supports multiple windows in a text screen, and makes a good editor for someone put off by the complexity of vi and doesn't want the size or extra features found in emacs.

Starting joe is simple, just type the command joe followed by the name of the file to edit.

```
> joe file.txt
```

You'll be placed into the editing window. The top line of the window has some information such as the name of the file and the command to get on-line help (that's CTRL-K followed by H). The remainder of the screen is the file to be edited. Unlike an editor such as vi, where you have a command mode and an editing mode, joe has only one mode—editing. Extra commands are entered as sets of control key combinations, such as CTRL-K H for help.

Here are some of the other commands that exist for joe:

CTRL-K F   - Find a string. Enter the string to find, enter, then other options you want set for that search such as ignore case, backwards search (instead of forwards) or a replace (to perform a search and replace).

CTRL-K L   - Go to a specific line in the file.

CTRL-Y   - Delete an entire line.

CTRL-K B   - Mark the start of a block at the current cursor loacation. As the cursor moves, the block will not be shown on the screen until you mark the end of the block with the end of block command (see below). If the end of the block is before the start of the block, the block will not be defined.

CTRL-K K   - Mark the end of the block at the current cursor location. This point has to be after the start of the block. Once you enter this sequence, and you have a valid block, it will become high-lighted. To remove the highlighting, move the cursor to the start of the block (or before it in the file) and mark the end of the block.

CTRL-K Y   - Delete the marked block.

CTRL-K M   - Move the marked block to the current cursor location.

CTRL-K W   - Write the marked block to a file. You will get prompted for a file-name.

CTRL-K X   - Save and quit.

CTRL-C   - Quit without saving. If the file has changed at all, you'll be asked if you're sure you want to quit.

Diff

One of the possible ways to upgrade your Linux kernel is through the use of patch files. These patch files are not a complete Linux kernel, but merely contain the differences between two versions. If I wanted to upgrade my Linux kernel from 1.3.95 to 1.3.96, I could download a 3.0MB file. This would take about 30–45 minutes on my modem. I could download a 20k patch file which would take under a minute. Using the patch file would make my kernel source code exactly the same as the 1.3.96 kernel source code.

The program used to create the patch files is called 'diff'. Diff will allow you to compare two files and not only tell you if they're different, but display the lines that are different in the two versions.

Let's take two files: `filea.txt` and `fileb.txt`:

`filea.txt`:

The Linux operating system, a UNIX-like project started by Linus Torvalds in Helsinki, Finland, is a powerful operating system. It can do anything except wash your dishes for you.

```
fileb.txt:
```

The Linux operating system, a UNIX-ish project started by Linus Torvalds in Helsinki, Finland, is a powerful operating system. It can do anything except wash your dishes for you.

The only arguments diff really needs are the two files you want to compare:

```
diff from-file to-file
> diff filea.txt fileb.txt
1c1
< The Linux operating system, a UNIX-like project started by
--
> The Linux operating system, a UNIX-ish project started by
>
```

Let's look at the output. The two lines which contain the only difference are printed. They are prefaced by either a greater-than (>) or a less-than sign (<). Lines prefaced with a < mean that it is the line that is different in the 'from-file,' which is `filea.txt` in our case. Lines prefaced with a >, then, are lines that are from the "to-file," which is `fileb.txt`. The `1c1` means that the first line in each file is different. Had the second line been different in each file, it would have read `2c2`.

The advantage to diff is that it allows you to set up a simple method of storing changes to source code files to other text files. By storing the diff output to a file, you can convert the from-file to the to-file:

```
> diff filea.txt fileb.txt > patch.fil
> patch < patch.fil
Hmm... Looks like a normal diff to me...
File to patch: filea.txt
Patching file filea.txt using Plan A...
Hunk #1 succeeded at 1.
done
> cat filea.txt
The Linux operating system, a UNIX-ish project started by
Linus Torvalds in Helsinki, Finland, is a powerful operating
system. It can do anything except wash your dishes for you.
> cat fileb.txt
```

```
The Linux operating system, a UNIX-ish project started by
Linus Torvalds in Helsinki, Finland, is a powerful operating
system. It can do anything except wash your dishes for you.
>
```

When you use patch to patch files, the originals are kept. The filename is almost the same, with the exception that in most cases a .orig will be added to the end of the name. So I now have filea.txt and filea.txt.orig. The filea.txt.orig file contains filea.txt as it existed before I patched it:

```
> cat filea.txt.orig
The Linux operating system, a UNIX-like project started by
Linus Torvalds in Helsinki, Finland is a powerful operating
system. It can do anything except wash your dishes for you.
>
```

The patch files for the kernel are slightly different. The kernel patch files contain more than just the line numbers that changed, but two lines on either side of the patch. This is so that the patch command can be sure that the lines it is inserting are the right ones.

CHAPTER
8

What Happens when Linux Boots?

Linux has at least three different ways to start. All involve rebooting the machine. First, you can have your root Linux partition be the 'active' partition in the BIOS and it is therefore booted when the machine gets turned on. This is the same way DOS gets booted in other machines. Next, you can have the kernel on a floppy disk, and while rebooting, insert the diskette into the drive, hope you have the BIOS set to detect drive A, and let the kernel boot off the diskette. Third, you can have a boot manager like LILO (LInux LOader) or the OS/2 Boot Manager allow you to select what operating system to start. In any case, once the kernel begins loading itself into memory, the end result is the same: a working Linux system.

As the kernel boots, you will see numerous messages fly across the screen. Some are for informational purposes (such as the BogoMips rating) and others are to help you in case a particular part of the kernel doesn't work as expected. For example, if you selected the wrong IRQ for your sound card, it could take you hours to trace the problem. Linux will tell you what devices it found, what IRQ it thinks the devices are on, and other information to help you determine the cause of the problem.

Once you are able to log in, you can use the `dmesg` command to display the kernel messages that were shown on boot. You may want to redirect the output to a file, or pipe it to `more`, as there will be more than a screen worth of output. Here's what my output looks like:

```
LILO: linux
```
>> I entered 'linux' to tell LILO to look up its entry for linux and start
>> it. With my setup, I could have also entered 'dos' or 'linux.old'
>> which starts MS-DOS or an older linux kernel respectively.

```
Uncompressing Linux.....................................done
```
>> The "Uncompressing Linux......done" message is here because the kernel
>> was getting too big for boot managers like LILO to handle, so the kernel
>> is compressed using the gzip algorithm, along with some code to allow the
>> kernel to uncompress itself when it boots.

```
Console: colour EGA+ 80x25, 1 virtual console (max 63)

bios32_init : BIOS32 Service Directory structure at 0x000fc310 bios32_init :
BIOS32 Service Directory entry at 0xfc740

pcibios_init : PCI BIOS revision 2.00 entry at 0xfc770

Probing PCI hardware.

Calibrating delay loop.. ok - 50.08 BogoMips
```
>> BogoMips are not a real indication of how fast the processor is.
>> It is used internally by the system for some timing loops.
>> Since different processors have different loops, this number will
>> change based on the CPU speed and type you have. There are some
>> Pentium processors that have a lower BogoMips rating than my
>> 486-based system, even though the Pentium is faster;
>> hence the 'bogo' (for bogus) in BogoMips.

```
Serial driver version 4.11 with no serial options enabled

tty00 at 0x03f8 (irq = 4) is a 16550A

tty01 at 0x02f8 (irq = 3) is a 16550A

lp1 at 0x0378, using polling driver

snd2 <SoundBlaster Pro 3.2> at 0x220 irq 7 drq 1

snd1 <Yamaha OPL-3 FM> at 0x388 irq 0 drq 0

hda: WDC AC2120M, 119MB w/32KB Cache, CHS=872/8/35, MaxMult=8

ide0: primary interface on irq 14

Floppy drive(s): fd0 is 1.44M, fd1 is 1.2M

FDC 0 is a post-1991 82077

scsi-ncr53c7,8xx : at PCI bus 0, device 1, function 0

scsi-ncr53c7,8xx : warning : revision of 2 is greater than 1.

scsi-ncr53c7,8xx : NCR53c810 at memory 0xfbfef000, io 0xe800, irq 9

scsi0 : using io mapped access

scsi0 : using initiator ID 7

scsi0 : using level active interrupts

scsi0 : burst length 8

scsi0 : using 40MHz SCSI clock

scsi0 : NCR code relocated to 0x1df150

scsi0 : test 1 started
```

```
scsi0 : NCR53c{7,8}xx (rel 4)
scsi : 1 host.
   Vendor: FUJITSU Model:. M2684S-512     Rev: 2035
   Type:    Direct-Access              ANSI SCSI revision:   02
Detected scsi disk sda at scsi0, id 0, lun 0
scsi : detected 1 SCSI disk total.
SCSI Hardware sector size is 512 bytes on device sda
Memory: 15008k/16384k available (672k kernel code, 384k reserved, 320k data)
This processor honours the WP bit even when in supervisor mode. Good.
Swansea University Computer Society NET3.019
Swansea University Computer Society TCP/IP for NET3.019
IP Protocols: ICMP, UDP, TCP
PPP: version 0.2.7 (4 channels) NEW_TTY_DRIVERS OPTIMIZE_FLAGS
TCP compression code copyright 1989 Regents of the University of California
PPP line discipline registered.
3c503.c:v1.10 9/23/93 Donald Becker (becker@cesdis.gsfc.nasa.gov)
eth0: 3c503 at 0x300, 02 60 8c 3c 53 9a
eth0: 3C503 using programmed I/O (REJUMPER for SHARED MEMORY).
Checking 386/387 coupling... Ok, fpu using exception 16 error reporting.
Checking 'hlt' instruction... Ok.
Linux version 1.2.9 (root@trippy) (gcc version 2.6.2) #5 Tue Jun 13 21:40:56
EDT 1995
Partition check:
   sda: sda1 sda2 sda3 sda4 < sda5 sda6 sda7 >
   hda: hda1 hda2
VFS: Mounted root (ext2 filesystem).
Adding Swap: 16312k swap-space
EXT2-fs warning: mounting unchecked fs, running e2fsck is recommended
EXT2-fs warning: mounting unchecked fs, running e2fsck is recommended
```

>> The above two statements are not as bad as you think. The EXT2
>> filesystem has a bit that can be set for 'checked' or 'unchecked.' When
>> the filesystem is unmounted correctly, the bit gets set to 'checked.'
>> But in some cases, the /sbin/shutdown program may not unmount the
>> partition and set the bit to checked, and thus the warning.
>> One case that would cause this is if the root user is in a mounted
>> directory. Since shutdown can't unmount the directory the user is logged
>> in, it doesn't get the 'clean' bit set. When you shutdown the system,
>> be sure the root user is in the root directory.

Once the kernel is booted and the root partition is mounted, the `/etc/init` process is started. This picks up where the kernel left off, mounting devices, starting more processes, allowing users to log in, and so on.

Init

After the Linux kernel boots, it needs a way of knowing what to do; much like MS-DOS needs a `config.sys` and `autoexec.bat`.

The init program handles a lot of functions (including making sure that your modem can be used for dialing into), sets up the getty processes on the Linux console, and also handles special events such as power failure and a user pressing the CTRL-ALT-DEL sequence. In addition, the init process makes sure that once a user logs out of the modem or the console, another user can immediately log in from the same place.

The kernel passes to the init process one option—the run-level to start in. The run-level is similar to the way DOS 6.0 and above have multiple boot sequences. Linux is limited to a total of ten different run-levels. Of these ten, a few are reserved for special, but sometimes uncommon, uses. The init process reads `/etc/inittab` and finds out which run-level to use, based on the defaults in the file. Init then starts the system up in that run-level. To change the run-level for a specific boot, you must be using LILO.

The ten run-levels are comprised of the numbers 0–6, and the letters A, B, C, and S. The seven numbers relate to the common methods of booting the kernel. Run-level 0 is usually used for shutting down, run-level 1 starts the system in single user mode, run-level 5 can be used to start the system in the X-Window System, and run-level 6 is used for rebooting. The remaining run-levels are left for whatever uses you want. The S run-level is special as it tells init to start up in single user mode, just like run-level 1. That is, only the root user is allowed to log in, and no other filesystems (other than the root one) are mounted. This is used for situations such as filesystem corruption where you want all of the other users off the system so you can test. The A, B, and C run-levels allow you to combine run-levels. You can be in run-level 5 and then start up additional processes from run-level A at the same time. I'll explain more of that in a minute.

Depending on the installation you have (and version of init) the default run-levels and the purpose of the numbered run-levels may differ. Check the man-pages for init and inittab for more information about your particular setup.

The Entries in Inittab

An entry in `/etc/inittab` looks like this:

```
id:runlevels:action:process
```

And anything between a # and the end of the line is treated as a comment.

Also, note the following for an understanding of this entry:

id   - A unique two-character identification for the entry.

runlevels - What run-levels to start the process under. There can be more than one entry in here, so to start a process under all conditions, you could have an entry like 0123456S

action   - This tells init how to handle the following process. Some actions are run no matter what the run-levels are, so watch out.

ACTIONS:

respawn   - If the process stops, restart it. This is for the getty and other processes that watch the serial or console ports awaiting logins.

wait   - init will start the process and wait for it to finish before continuing with other entries. These should be short programs, since you'll have to wait until the process finishes to log in.

boot   - Runs when the system boots. This action ignores the run-level field.

bootwait   - This is a combination of boot and wait. Init executes the process on bootup, and waits for it to finish before continuing. This entry ignores the run-level field.

sysinit   - Runs during the system boot and is done before any boot or bootwait entries.

ondemand   - This is where the A, B, and C run-levels come in. This specifies that if this run-level is entered, the process starts but no change in the current run-level is performed.

initdefault - This tells init what the default run-level is. This should be one of the first lines in the inittab file. The run-level field should have only one entry—the run-level to start out in.

ctrlaltdel   - When a user sitting at the console hits the CTRL-ALT-DEL sequence; this entry contains by default a safe shutdown.

process   - The process to run. This can be shell scripts or compiled programs. As we'll soon see, using shell scripts for much of the boot sequence is preferable to having many entries in /etc/inittab.

Here's what part of my inittab looks like. Note that the entries in init are started (if they're started) in order in the file. So you would want to put your getty and other interface statements last so the system has a chance to boot completely.

```
id:5:initdefault:
   # Default run-level
si:S:sysinit:/etc/rc.d/rc.S
   # System initialization (runs when system boots).
su:S:wait:/etc/rc.d/rc.K
   # Script to run when going single user.
rc:123456:wait:/etc/rc.d/rc.M
   # Script to run when going multi-user.
ca::ctrlaltdel:/sbin/shutdown -t3 -rf now
   # What to do at the "Three Finger Salute".
c1:12345:respawn:/sbin/agetty 38400 tty1

c2:12345:respawn:/sbin/agetty 38400 tty2

c3:45:respawn:/sbin/agetty 38400 tty3

c4:45:respawn:/sbin/agetty 38400 tty4

c5:45:respawn:/sbin/agetty 38400 tty5

c6:456:respawn:/sbin/agetty 38400 tty6
```

<< Here is where the agetty processes are started for each virtual console.
<< In this case, I have a total of six VCs that I can log into. Since the
<< kernel has support for eight VCs by default (and you can code in up to
<< sixty-four VCs if you like), you can access those VCs by simply adding in more
<< agetty lines. Since the agetty processes take up memory, and I
<< do not need more than six VCs at a time, I leave it alone.
<< To add an entry for tty7, to give you a total of seven VCs that you can log
<< into, make an entry like this:
<< c7:45:respawn:/sbin/agetty 38400 tty7
<< and you can either reboot, or use the telinit program (which I explain
<< later) to change the run-level.

```
#s1:45:respawn:/sbin/agetty 19200 ttyS0

#s2:45:respawn:/sbin/agetty 19200 ttyS1
   # Serial lines
#d1:45:respawn:/sbin/agetty -mt60 38400,19200,9600,2400,1200 ttyS0

#d2:45:respawn:/sbin/agetty -mt60 38400,19200,9600,2400,1200 ttyS1
   # Dialup lines
#f1:45:respawn:/usr/local/sbin/mgetty -R 60 ttyS1
   # Fax line
```

<< If I had a fax or dialin line that I wanted to use, I could uncomment
<< the above lines, depending on the serial port I was using.

```
x1:6:wait:/etc/rc.d/rc.6
   # Run-level 6 used to be for an X-window only system, until we discovered
   # that it throws init into a loop that keeps your load average at least 1 all
   # the time. Thus, there is now one getty opened on tty6. Hopefully no one
   # will notice. ;^)
   # It might not be bad to have one text console anyway, in case something
   # happens to X.
```

<< And here's run-level 6

The ability exists within init to change the run-level on the fly; either to immediately test changes, or to start up access on your serial port without rebooting the entire system. The telinit program is used to do this:

```
# telinit <rl>
```

Where `<rl>` is the run-level you wish to change to. It may take a few moments to run, but once it is completed, you will be in the new run-level and your new programs will be started. In an emergency situation, you can drop the system to run-level S (the single user mode) by entering

```
# telinit S
```

Once the crisis has passed (you fixed the hard drive, the crackers left, the phone system becomes available, and so on) you can restore the old run-level allowing other users access by entering

```
# telinit 5
```

rc Files

The `rc` files, which are used by Linux and started via the init process, are all located in the `/etc/rc.d` directory by default. This way, all of the startup commands are found in the same directory.

A typical installation will have the following files:

rc.0   - Script to run during shutdown; usually just turns off any swap space and umounts all partitions except root

rc.6   - Script to run at run-level 6 (to start X)

rc.K   - Brings the system down to single user mode (kill the system)

rc.S   - Runs at boot time—mounts devices, checks drives, then runs

rc.serial - (Start the system)

rc.M   - Run after rc.S, it starts the network (in rc.inet1 and rc.inet2), prepares the system for multi-users, then executes any local commands in rc.local

rc.serial - Initializes all available serial ports. You may want to modify this if you have a multiport serial card or if you have a high-speed modem.

rc.local - This is the best place to put commands local to your machine; commands like setting the clock for your particular timezone, starting any additional daemons, and so on.

rc.inet1   - Sets up the initial routing and TCP/IP interfaces needed to use TCP/IP. This is where the IP address, network address, netmask, and other variables needed by TCP/IP are set.

rc.inet2   - Starts programs needed for TCP/IP, such as inetd, syslogd, and any other programs such as mounting NFS drives, name server daemon, and so on.

For most setups, you will not have to modify these files, with the exception of `rc.local`, `rc.serial`, and `rc.inet1` and `rc.inet2`. Also, some of these files have programs to configure them. For example, the netconfig program with Slackware distributions will configure the `rc.inet1` file, while the general install program will set up portions of `rc.serial`. Your `rc.local` file may be empty, and is just fine to stay that way. If you know what you are doing with TCP/IP and wish to have additional services started up (like NFS, named, routed) you can uncomment out the appropriate lines in `rc.inet2`. You can also create `rc.[1-5]` files to run when entering a specific run-level. Create the file to run whatever extra programs you wish to run and add an entry in the `/etc/inittab` that looks something like this:

```
r1:1:wait:/etc/rc.d/rc.1
```

One interesting thing to note about the `rc` files is that they are executed after the kernel has started, and therefore many of the commands in the files can be run by hand as root user. For example, if you were debugging network problems, and needed to change the sections of your TCP/IP configuration, you can execute the appropriate commands to turn the network interface off, modify the `rc.inet1` file, then execute it. Be aware that executing some `rc` files (such as `rc.M`) can execute other `rc` files.

Getty

Once the init is completed, it starts up the getty processes. Getty monitors a particular port to see if there is a request to go out of the port or if a login request is coming in the port. It sets up lock files so that no two processes can use the same port at the same time. It would cause a conflict if one program tried to send a fax out through a modem that someone is logged in on. Getty is also the process that answers the modem when a call comes in.

There are many different versions of getty, some better suited to tasks than others. For example, while plain getty is good for simple tasks like handling the console, it is not as good as agetty for handling modems and other serial ports. If you're using a fax modem and want to be able to send and receive faxes, there is another version of getty for that as well. Most of these versions come preinstalled on the system, so when I refer to getty it can mean either getty itself or any of its variants.

The entries in /etc/inittab for agetty have the line speed and terminal name as arguments. For the console this should be set to 38400 and the name of the terminal. This is really a filename in the /dev directory. Since agetty assumes that all devices are in the /dev directory, there is no need to prefix each device with /dev/. The serial ports have the -mt60 option:

-m—Guess the line speed based on what the modem returns to getty. Most modems send a string like CONNECT 14400 when it connects to a remote modem (or when a remote modem connects to it). Agetty uses this since it is faster and more convenient to use than the other method of finding the speed, waiting for the user to press the <ENTER> key, and then computing the port speed.

-t60—Wait sixty seconds for a user to type in their username, then if no username is given within sixty seconds, hang up the line.

The list of numbers after the -mt60 refer to what speeds the modem should be able to pick up on. This handles the standard modem lines of 38400 through 1200. If you wish to change this (for example, you don't want anyone dialing in at 1200 bps on your shiny new 28.8k modem), you can remove the entries in the line. Getty will cycle through the modem speeds, and if it doesn't connect at a speed in the list, it drops the connection.

If a connection is made, it reads the login name, then passes this information to the login program, which then prompts the user for his or her password. At this point, there are a few important things to note:

1. The password is sent to the remote machine, but not echoed back. This means that the user typing in the password will not be able to see it, but someone who may be monitoring the port (either through phone tapping, Ethernet snooping, or other methods) can still capture the password. There are methods of sending the password securely such as Kerberos.

2. The password in /etc/passwd is encrypted. The password that is sent is encrypted, then compared to the password field in /etc/passwd. If the two encrypted passwords match, then the login program starts the user's shell. If the passwords do not match, the user must re-enter the username and password. If the user fails to enter the password three times, the login program will drop the connection and the user will have to dial back into the machine to log in.

CHAPTER
9

- Environment Variables

- Using the Shell

- Shell Functions

Fun with Shells

The two main shells for Linux are the tcsh (C-shell) and bash (for Bourne Again Shell, a variation on the original Bourne shell). Since Linux uses tcsh instead of sh, and bash instead of sh, each of these shells are the same. That is, you should be able to do anything you can in sh using bash instead.

Other shells include the kshell and zshell, which include a bit more functionality and slightly different programming structures.

Environment Variables

Just like in DOS, sh and csh support environment variables. These variables allow you to set certain options or other variables needed for the user to use the shell correctly. The most common variable you'll see is the path variable, just like you see in DOS. This path tells the shell which directories to examine to load a program. There is, however, one significant difference between the DOS and sh(csh) shells. DOS will check the current working directory for an executable program by default. Because of security concerns, sh won't check the current working directory by default. So you'll have to remember to do one of two things:

1.   Add the current working directory (as a .) to the path statement

2.   If you want to run a program that is not in the path, preface the program with ./. So you'd have a command line that looks like this:

```
>  ./command

>
```

You can set a variable in two ways. The most common way is to use the set command:

91

```
$ set PATH=/usr/bin:/bin:.
$ set | grep PATH
PATH (/usr/bin /bin .)
$
```

The csh shell uses the `setenv` command to set environment variables. One note about `setenv` is that it does not require the equal character as the set command does in sh. You give the `setenv` command, the variable to set, and what you want it set equal to. Remember to make sure the variable is in capital letters:

```
> setenv PATH /usr/bin:/bin:.
> setenv | grep PATH
PATH=/usr/bin:/bin:.
>
```

Since a lot of programs use or even require environment variables to be set, listed are a few of the variables, what programs use them, and what the variable contains:

var Name	Command	How Used
LESS	less	Treats the contents of this variable as flags given on the command line. This allows you to have a customized less setup and then just type 'less \<filename>' and the options get passed.

Sample:

```
> setenv LESS -EM
```

Provides for exiting the less program the first time it reaches the end of the file (without having to type 'Q') and provides extra information about the file at the bottom of the screen.

MANPATH	man	Contains a list of default directories to search that contain either `man[1-9]` or `cat[1-9]` directories underneath.

Sample:

```
> setenv MANPATH /usr/man:/usr/local/man
```

DISPLAY	X programs	Contains the hostname and the display to use to send X related data to. This allows you to run an X program on one machine and have the program actually output on another machine.

Sample:

```
> setenv DISPLAY trippy.wizvax.net:0.0
```

For most cases, you can just set this to <host>:0.0 since the 0.0 is used when you have multiple instances of X running on one machine and multiple displays on that machine. Programs like Xnest or the virtual consoles feature of Linux allow more than one X session to run at once. Also make sure that the <host> is set to the machine you are currently running the X server from (We'll get into X in a few chapters).

EDITOR	Many user progams (like less)	Contains the name of the default editor to run when you want to edit a file. This allows you to use your favorite editor. It usually defaults to /usr/bin/vi.

Sample:

```
> setenv EDITOR /usr/bin/joe
```

TERM	Most programs	Contains the terminal type that you are currently using. This is usually defined when you start the shell up, and may not need to be changed or set. The terminal type for the Linux console is console.

Sample:

```
> setenv TERM console
```

Using the Shell

Now that you're in the shell and you've been using it for a while, it is time to learn about some of the key commands the shell uses to do its job. For example, both the tcsh and bash have command line histories. This enables you to not only scroll through previous commands, but interactively edit and rerun a command. If you misspell a particularly long command line, you can just hit the up-arrow key and your command will be displayed again. Use the right- and left-arrow keys to move the cursor along the line.

To make using the shell even easier, the keys have what are known as bindings, which allow you to map a particular key to an action. For example, if you type CTRL-A at a shell prompt, the cursor will jump to the beginning of the line. These bindings allow you to remap keys to your liking. The optimal way to remap the keys is to make it more like your favorite editor. To make the bindings easier for users, many shells come with premade bindings for vi and emacs users. Someone who is familiar with many of the key setups for vi or emacs can quickly become familiar with the key bindings for tcsh or bash.

Here are a few of the key bindings that are shared between the two (that is, both emacs and vi use these bindings). In these examples, the control key is replaced with a carat (^) and the alt key is replaced with an M (for Meta). Since many other UNIX keyboards do not have control or alt keys (the DEC vt220 keyboard doesn't have an alt key for example), the Meta key is a keyboard-independent key.

^A   Move the cursor to the beginning of the line

^C   Send a SIGINTR (interrupt) to the shell

^D   Show list (see ^I for a better explanation)

^E   Move to end of line

^K   Kill from the cursor position to the end of the line

^N   Move down in the history list (N for next)

^P   Move up in the history list (P for previous)

^U   Kill the entire line, regardless of cursor position

^I   Filename completion. This is also the tab key, and allows you to complete the name of an executable if it's the first word on the line, or a file in the current directory if it's the second or after word in the line.

If I wanted to run the `mkdir` command, but I could not spell it (or was just lazy), I could type

```
> mkd
```

then hit the ^I key and I'd see

```
> mkdir
```

If I wanted to remove a directory in the current directory called `directory_I_want_to_delete`, I could type something like this:

```
> rmdir direct
```

I could hit the ^I key which would give me:

```
> rmdir directory_I_want_to_delete
```

In a case where there is more than one file that starts with the same characters, the shell will put in as many characters as it can, then beep, informing you that there are other possibilities. Let's say I added a directory called `directory_I_want_to_keep`. Using the above example, I'd have

```
> rmdir direct(^I)
> rmdir directory_I_want_to_
```

At this point, I can either type in k (for keep) or d (for delete) and hit the ^I key again. Or, I just can hit ^D, and get a list of all the files in the current directory that begin with those characters:

```
> rmdir directory_I_want_to_(^D)
directory_I_want_to_delete directory_I_want_to_keep
> rmdir directory_I_want_to_
```

This is a very handy feature, especially for long filenames, directories, or when you don't remember the exact spelling of a file or directory.

You're probably wondering how to change or set the key bindings. The csh shell has the `bindkey` or `bind` command which allows you to change or set key bindings. The bindings allow you to map a specific key to either a csh function or it can run a macro. You could map ^O to `2>& err.out` to allow you to redirect STDERR of a command to a file called `err.out` merely by hitting ^O at the end of your command line.

The bash shell uses the `bind` command, which has similar functionality to csh's `bindkey` command. The default bindings are again for emacs, and you can get a listing of the current bindings using the `bind -v` command. You can switch between mappings using the `bind -m <map>` command, where map can be any of: vi, emacs, or other variations on the emacs and vi keys.

Bash also has the ability to load a specified file on startup to set the mappings for you. By default it's called `~/.inputrc`, otherwise, it checks the file in the INPUTRC environment variable. One feature of the `bind` command is that it will output all the current bindings in `.inputrc` format using the `bind -l` command. You could then redirect the output of the `bind` command to the `.inputrc` file and edit it from there. The format of the `.inputrc` is like this:

keyname: function

keyname: "macro"

Where:

keyname: A key sequence, such as Control-O, Meta-O, or Control-Meta-O.

function: A function supported by the bash shell. A list of functions are available by using the `bind -l` command from bash. The bash manual (man bash) also contains a listing of the available functions, and the default mapping.

"macro": Text you want to output when the keyname is pressed.

Shell Functions

Just like other programming languages, the bash shell (and the sh shell) has some rather powerful functions. Programming these functions into files which are then executed create shell scripts.

Shell scripts are merely a collection of commands and programs put together. It is very similar to a DOS `.BAT` file, except that the shell scripts have much greater functionality. There are a few reasons for this. First, there are hundreds of commands avilable in UNIX as opposed to the tens that are available in DOS. Second, most of the UNIX programs support piping and redirection. Many DOS programs will not accept data from a pipe or can redirect their output to a file. In UNIX, this is replaced with switches that provide the program with all of the information it needs when it starts. Third, there are more scripting commands available in sh, making it more of a true programming language (with if..then..else, for, and while loops).

You can use the features of shell scripting from the command line. To do this, be sure you're running the bash shell (you can type sh to be sure).

```
bash$ for i in *
> do
> ls -ld $i
> done
```

This is the same as typing `ls -ld *`. The difference is that this shell script is slower, since `ls` has to be called for each file. This constant restart of the `ls` program, instead of a single start for `ls -ld *`, makes the shell script slower.

To make this an actual script (something that the shell reads in and then executes) you can use your favorite text editor to make a file that looks like this:

```
for i in *
do
ls -ld $1
done
```

Save it as `direct.sh`:

```
> chmod +x direct.sh
> direct.sh
```

The for loop has a general syntax of

```
for <variable> in <list>
do
<command>
...
done
```

where:

<variable>—A string that starts with an alphabetic or underscore character, and is followed by zero or more numbers, letters, or underscore characters.

<list>—A list of items. This list can be separated by spaces and can contain wildcard characters (* and ?). Note, however, that items in the list with wild-

card characters will try to match up with filenames in the current working directory.

<command>—A list of commands. If you want to access items in the list, put a $ in front of the variable name. You'll see above that the variable is called i, but when the script tries to use the value of the variable, it uses it as $i.

One thing to keep in mind when writing shell scripts is the possible outcome of the script. Let's take the above shell script. The usual command for getting a directory listing is ls -la. If I were to use ls -la in the shell script, or even ls -l, I wouldn't get the same output. I would get not only a directory listing of all the files in the directory, but also a directory listing of each subdirectory. Why? If you run ls -l on a directory entry, you'll get a listing of files within that directory. The -d flag tells ls to ignore files that exist in the directory and just display the directory entry.

There's also if..then(..else), while..do, and until..do statements, among others. The formats for these statements are similar to the for..do loop. One other conditional you can use for these statements is the test command. Test allows you to test for various conditions such as:

a file exists

a file exists and has certain bits set

a file exists and is executable

one file is bigger (or older) than another

equality of variables (or strings)

Test returns a 0 for a false statement, and a 1 for a true statement. If a file called direct.sh exists, then a statement like

```
bash$ if test -e direct.sh
> then
> echo "file exists"
> fi
```

would return

```
file exists
bash$
```

Another way of testing is to enclose the test options in [ ] characters. So the above command could also be written as

```
bash$ if [ -e direct.sh ]
> then
```

```
> echo "file exists"
> fi
```

Other options to test include:

`-d <file>`	- `<file>` is a directory
`-w <file>`	- `<file>` is writable
`<string>`	- `<string>` is not null
`<string1> = <string2>`	- `<string1>` is identical to `<string2>`
`! <expr>`	- `<expr>` is false
`<expr1> -a <expr2>`	- `<expr1>` and `<expr2>` are true
`<expr1> -o <expr2>`	- `<expr1>` or `<expr2>` are true

The `if` command has a structure of:

```
if <condition>
then
<command>
...
fi
```

Actually in this case, the condition is a bit more than using test. For example, you can have a `grep` command:

```
if who | grep mfk
then
echo "mfk is logged on"
fi
```

Now the output from this is a bit different than what you would expect:

```
mfk       tty1      Oct 30 19:07
mfk       ttyp1     Oct 30 19:25 (:0.0)
mfk       ttyp2     Oct 30 19:27 (:0.0)
mfk is logged on
bash$
```

The reason for this is that the shell is sending the output of the `who` and `grep` command to STDOUT. We can prevent the extra output by making the command be something more like

```
if who | grep mfk > /dev/null
then
echo "mfk is logged on"
fi
```

And the output is

```
mfk is logged on
bash$
```

The while..do structure is of the form:

```
while <condition>
do
<command>
. . .
done
```

The until..do looks like this:

```
until <condition>
do
<command>
. . .
done
```

For those of you familiar with C, there is also a case statement:

```
case <value> in
        <val1> )  command
                  command
                  . . .
                  command ;;
        <val2> )  command
                  command
                  . . .
                  command ;;
        . . .
        <valn> )  command
                  command
                  . . .
                  command ;;
esac
```

where <value> is the variable to be checked and <val1>..<valn> are the possible values of that variable. If you include * as the last value, it becomes the default command to run.

CHAPTER 10

Handling Devices

As in the Windows Control panel, Linux allows you to have control over the hardware in your system. This control is more extensive than what is available in Windows and DOS, as you are actually able to make devices unavailable if you want. In Windows, if you create a FAT drive, it gets assigned a drive letter and becomes available, whether you want it or not. Windows NT provides the ability to mount or not mount drives, so NT is closer to Linux in this respect. In fact,with the right software and user setups, you could control access to most aspects of your hardware; from controlling the sound card to dialing out via the modem.

While accessing and controlling hardware devices is not as easy as the Windows Control panel, it is quite flexible and requires little maintenance once it is set up. In some cases you have to recompile the kernel if you want to add new hardware to your system. CD-ROMs and sound cards will probably require this. Using devices like a modem, mice, or hard drives does not usually require rebuilding the kernel, and much of it can be done without rebooting the system.

Hard Drives

The hard drive in other PC-based operating systems has to be partitioned before you can actually format it. DOS has fdisk, and so does Linux. Unlike the DOS version, however, you are able to create different partition types. Each partition has an ID associated with it which tells the OS what kind of partition it is. This is what prevents DOS from trying to use an HPFS or NTFS or even ext2fs partition as a FAT partition. DOS only looks for FAT partitions, OS/2 looks for FAT and HPFS partitions and so on. The Linux fdisk gives you the ability to change or modify these IDs, so be sure you know what you're doing. To extend some more security to fdisk, you must be the root user to use it.

That said, let's look at fdisk:

```
> su
Passwd:
bash# fdisk
Using /dev/hda as default device!

Command (m for help):
```

This is what you'll probably see when you start fdisk. If you are using only SCSI drives, the hda will be replaced with sda. If you wish to use a different physical disk, enter it right after fdisk:

```
bash# fdisk /dev/hdb
```

Back to the prompt. We can get help on some of the fdisk commands by entering a question mark (?) at the prompt:

```
Command (m for help): ?

Command action
    a    toggle a bootable flag
    d    delete a partition
    l    list known partition types
    m    print this menu
    n    add a new partition
    p    print the partition table
    q    quit without saving changes
    t    change a partition's system id
    u    change display/entry units
    v    verify the partition table
    w    write table to disk and exit
    x    extra functionality (experts only)

Command (m for help):
```

Let's use the p command to see what partitions we have already:

```
Command (m for help): p

Disk /dev/hda: 8 heads, 35 sectors, 872 cylinders
Units = cylinders of 280 * 512 bytes

    Device Boot  Begin  Start   End  Blocks   Id  System
/dev/hda1    *      1      1    183  25602+    4  DOS 16-bit <32M
/dev/hda2         184    184    872  96460    83  Linux native

Command (m for help):
```

Here you can see some statistics about the disk that Linux was able to find, along with a table of the partitions on the physical disk. The first column has the device entry in /dev for the partition. The second column indicates whether the partition is marked active or not. The active partition is the one that gets booted by the machine when it first starts. Only the first IDE hard drive or the frist SCSI hard drive can be set bootable.

The next column shows where that partition begins. The PC architecture will only allow four partitions per drive, but one of these partitions can be created as an extended partition. An extended partition allows you to have more partitions within it.

The next two columns show the start and end cylinders of the partitions. In the first line of output, it shows that the drive has a total of 872 cylinders. If you look at the start and end cylinders for both partitions, you see that partition one starts at cylinder 1 and goes to cylinder 183, and partition two starts at cylinder 184 and ends at 872. This shows that the entire hard drive is used up.

The sixth column shows the number of 1k blocks used by the partition. The first partition is about 25MB, and the second partition is about 96MB. The + next to the first partition shows that a minor amount of space is being wasted. This is because cylinders don't exactly match to 1k blocks. In the case where a cylinder fills up the last 1k block plus some extra space that is smaller than 1k, that space does not get used by Linux.

The ID in the second to last column shows the ID number of the partition. This relates to the ID number I mentioned earlier. The last column shows in a format, readable by humans, what that ID means. Here, ID 4 means a DOS partition that is smaller than 32MB (since it's only 25MB). ID 83 relates to a Linux partition of some kind. Note that the partition ID won't always tell you what filesystem type is actually on the partition. Nor does it mean that the partition is formatted at all. It merely tells the OS that looks at it what the drive expects to have on it. This prevents DOS from trying to use an ext2fs drive.

Let's create a new partition out of the extra space that is available.

```
Command (m for help): p
Disk /dev/hda: 8 heads, 35 sectors, 872 cylinders
Units = cylinders of 280 * 512 bytes
   Device Boot  Begin  Start  End  Blocks   Id  System
/dev/hda1    *       1      1  183  25602+    4  DOS 16-bit <32M
```

```
Command (m for help): n
Command action
   e    extended
   p    primary partition (1-4)
p
Partition number (1-4): 2
First cylinder (184-872): 184
Last cylinder or +size or +sizeM or +sizeK (184-872): 872

Command (m for help): p

Disk /dev/hda: 8 heads, 35 sectors, 872 cylinders
Units = cylinders of 280 * 512 bytes

   Device Boot  Begin  Start   End  Blocks   Id  System
/dev/hda1    *       1      1   183   25602+   4  DOS 16-bit <32M
/dev/hda2          184    184   872   96460   83  Linux native

Command (m for help):
```

I could tell how big I wanted to make the partition using two methods. First, I could see that fdisk reported I had 872 cylinders available to me, and that only 183 of them were being used. Second, when I created the partition, fdisk asked me what the ending cylinder would be. It also displayed two numbers. The first one is the minimum cylinder number, and the larger of the two is the highest cylinder number I could give. If I knew exactly how big I wanted the partition, say exactly 25MB, I could have entered in +25M instead of 872.

In the second partition listing, you can see that Linux created the partition and gave it a partition ID of Linux native. You can see what other partition types are available by giving fdisk the l command.

Here is a listing of the partition types that the Linux fdisk knows about.

```
Command (m for help): l

0  Empty            8   AIX          75  PC/IX         b8  BSDI swap
1  DOS 12-bit FAT   9   AIX bootable 80  Old MINIX     c7  Syrinx
2  XENIX root       a   OPUS         81  Linux/MINIX   db  CP/M
3  XENIX usr        40  Venix 80286  82  Linux swap    e1  DOS access
4  DOS 16-bit <32M  51  Novell?      83  Linux native  e3  DOS R/O
5  Extended         52  Microport    93  Amoeba        f2  DOS secondary
6  DOS 16-bit >=32  63  GNU HURD     94  Amoeba BBT    ff  BBT
7  OS/2 HPFS        64  Novell       b7  BSDI fs
Command (m for help):
```

In the next few months, an update for fdisk will probably contain information about the NTFS. The partition types that concern us here are types 81 through 83. These are the partition types that Linux knows natively. The first partition type (81) was used when Linux was still based on the Minix filesystem. Now that Linux is such a large project, it has its own partition type for Linux Native (ID 83). ID 82 is used to tell Linux that this partition is a swap partition and should be used for adding virtual memory to your system. Since we're using this partition for Linux, there's no need to change the ID type. The fdisk program already set it for us. Now let's save this partition:

```
Command (m for help): w
The partition table has been altered!
Calling BLKRRPART ioctl() to re-read partition table
Syncing disks
Reboot your system to ensure partition table is updated
bash#
```

Let's do what it says—reboot. It isn't required since Linux will reread the partition table, but better safe than sorry—especially when you're dealing with your data.

Now that the machine has rebooted, you can login as root and format the partition to a particular filesystem. The best choice for filesystem use is the ext2fs, since that's the most widely use filesystem type for Linux and the one that has gone under the most development.

MKFS

There are only three options you really need to give to mkfs:

`-t <fstype>` : Where `<fstype>` is ext, ext2, minix, xia - should be ext2

`-c`   : Tells mkfs to search for bad blocks, and mark them bad if found. It takes longer to format, but ensures against filesystem corruption later on.

`<device>`   : The partition you just created in fdisk. In this case, it's `/dev/hda2`.

Let's see the output from mkfs:

```
bash# mkfs -t ext2 -c /dev/hda2
mke2fs 0.5b, 11-Mar-95 for EXT2 FS 0.5a, 94/10/23
24192 inodes, 96460 blocks
```

```
4823 blocks (5.00%) reserved for the super user
First data block=1
Block size=1024 (log=0)
Fragment size=1024 (log=0)
12 block groups
8192 blocks per group, 8192 fragments per group
2016 inodes per group
Superblock backups stored on blocks:
        8193, 16385, 24577, 32769, 40961, 49153, 57345, 65537,
        73729, 81921, 90113
Checking for bad blocks (read-only test): done
Writing inode tables: done
Writing superblocks and filesystem accounting information: done
bash#
```

There are a few things to note in this output. On the third line of output you see that 5% of the filesystem is reserved for the root user. There are two reasons for allocating space to the root user. First, the algorithms for the ext2 filesystem make it rather hard for files to become fragmented as they do in DOS. That is, in DOS, a file can be literally scattered all over the drive. This makes access to the file slow since the hard drive heads have to move all over the place to find data. The ext2 filesystem tries to place each file in one block, making file access faster. In order to do this, the filesystem algorithm needs some amount of free space for it to prevent the fragmentation.

The second reason is just as practical: Root should have some sort of space available to it in the case of an emergency. For example, log files that root writes to could become truncated and lead to problems later on. As long as this is caught, there won't be many problems.

In either case, the amount of space lost (less than 5MB out of a 96MB filesystem) is minimal compared to the gains you get from having that space available to you.

One other point to note is the number of 'superblock backups' that mkfs created. The superblock is the single most important piece of data on your partition, since it contains data about the filesystem. Things like free space, file location, and other information are contained there. If the superblock gets corrupted, the partition becomes all but useless. Fortunately, the superblock has backups that get written to the partition about every 8M (or 8192 blocks). In the event of one superblock getting corrupted, there are backups waiting to be used by the fsck program.

FSCK— File System Check

Just like scandisk or chkdsk, Linux can check and repair possible damage to a filesystem. Corruption can come from many areas, but the most common is turning off the power to the machine without running shutdown. The ext2fs has flags built into the filesystem to tell if the filesystem was unmounted cleanly or not. When a proper shutdown occurs, the filesystem flag gets set to 'clean.' When the filesystem gets mounted, this flag gets set to 'dirty.' The next time the filesystem gets mounted, this flag gets checked. In the event that the flag is 'dirty,' you'll get a notice that the filesystem in question was not unmounted cleanly and should be checked.

The most common point where a filesystem will get mounted is during the boot process. If the mount command discovers that the filesystem is dirty, it will notify you. In some instances, fsck will automatically run for you.

Running fsck by hand requires that the filesystem is unmounted and that you have root access:

```
bash# fsck -t <fstype> <device>
```

where

`fstype` : The filesystem type, can be xia, ext, ext2, minix

`device` : Device entry, as it appears in fdisk (/dev/hda2)

If there is a severe problem with a filsystem and it won't mount, you'll have to run fsck by hand and try to repair the damage. If fsck can't repair the damage, this usually signals one of three things:

1.   The superblock got corrupted.

2.   There is a physical problem with the drive.

3.   You're using the wrong filesystem type.

Problem number two is rather serious and can't really be fixed through software.

Problem number three can be an annoyance, and can potentially be a problem if you work too hard at it. If you try and fix what you think is an ext2 filesystem when it is really a FAT filesystem, the FAT filesystem will be seriously corrupted by this. In the event where Linux tries reading a filesystem other than what you tell fsck it is, you'll see this:

```
bash# fsck -t minix /dev/hda2
fsck.minix: bad magic number in super-block
bash#
```

When in doubt, write down what filesystems you have, where they're located, and where they should be mounted. This will save a lot of headaches later on.

Problem one, however, can be fixed, since superblock backups are kept. The best place to begin looking is at block 8193, since this is likely to be the location of the first backup. The next location to look is 8193+8192=16385, and so on, until you find a copy of the superblock that works.

To tell fsck to use a different superblock, use the -b option to fsck:

```
fsck -t ext2 -b 8193 /dev/hda2
```

Mount

Now that our partition is set up, a filesystem is installed on it, and we know how to fix it if anything goes wrong, we can mount and begin using the filesystem. Doing this requires (you got it) root access and use of the `mount` command.

The syntax is rather simple:

```
bash# mount -t <fstype> <device> <mount-point>
```

where:

`fstype`	: Filesystem type
`device`	: Device as seen in fdisk
`mount-point`	: Location to mount the filesystem in

The only thing new here is the mount point. This is the directory that you want to mount the filesystem off of. Be sure the directory is otherwise empty, as the data in that directory isn't available after you mount something there. The data isn't gone, and you'll see it again when you unmount it. You just won't be able to access or see the data while that filesystem is mounted.

Mounting a CD-ROM or some other read-only device has an addition to the mount command:

```
bash# mount -t iso9660 -o ro <device> <mount-point>
```

The `iso9660` is used only if you're using a CD-ROM. SCSI CD-ROM drives have a device file of `/dev/sr0` and up. ATAPI and non-SCSI CD-ROM drives vary depending on the type of CD-ROM and the drivers it uses. The `-o ro` tells the kernel that the partition being mounted is a read-only device. When the kernel first boots, it mounts the root device read-only so that it can run fsck on it and the other partitions before completeing the boot sequence. Once the fsck is done, it remounts the root device as read-write.

Unmounting a partition is easier to do than mounting:

```
bash# umount <partition or directory>
```

Where the option can be either the partition you want to unmount, or the directory that it's mounted as. If no one else on the system is using the partition, that partition will get unmounted.

The Linux Loader (LILO)

A program you may have used when you installed your system is the Linux Loader or LILO. It allows you to select an operating system to boot when you turn on the machine. LILO is similar to the OS/2 Boot Manager in this respect. When LILO is installed, every time you boot your machine, you'll see a prompt like this:

```
LILO
```

In most setups, if you press any of the following keys:

Shift

Control

Alt

CapsLock

Scroll Lock

you enter the LILO command mode, and you can select an operating system to boot up. If you do not press the key, then the default operating system is started. The default operating system is the first one listed in LILO's table.

To install LILO, first make sure the program files are located on your machine. They will probably be in `/etc/lilo`, but could be just about anywhere. Use the command

```
> find / -name "lilo" -print
```

to find the location of the LILO directory. Then read the README file included there. One other source of information is the LILO-HOWTO located at sunsite.unc.edu, on numerous WWW sites, and probably on the CD-ROM you installed Linux from.

You can install LILO by running the `/sbin/liloconfig` program:

```
# /sbin/liloconfig
```

LILO Installation

LILO (the Linux Loader) is the program that allows you to boot Linux directly from the hard drive. To install, you make a new LILO configuration file by creating a new header and then adding at least one bootable partition to the file. Once you've done this, you can select the `install` option. Alternately, if you already have an `/etc/lilo.conf`, you may reinstall using that. If you make a mistake, just select (1) to start over.

Consider these options:

1—Start LILO configuration with a new LILO header

2—Add a Linux partition to the LILO config file

3—Add an OS/2 partition to the LILO config file

4—Add a DOS partition to the LILO config file

5—Install LILO

6—Reinstall LILO using the existing `lilo.conf`

7—Skip LILO installation and exit this menu

8—View your current `/etc/lilo.conf`

9—Read the Linux Loader HELP file

Which option would you like (1–9)?

The first option you will want is number 1—start LILO configuration. Once that is done, add in the partitions you want to boot using options 2, 3, and 4. Entering new partitions will allow you to give a name to each type. The name you enter for this is what you will need to enter to start that particular OS, so don't call your Linux partition, "My linux partition that's at kernel version 1.2.13" or else you'll do a lot of typing. Also be sure that each partition is actually bootable. In other words, make sure that the DOS drive you want to boot is the C: drive. Linux partitions should be the root partitions. After this is complete, use option 5 to install LILO. Once LILO is installed, you can reboot your system and see the LILO prompt.

To remove LILO, you must use the fdisk `/MBR` command in MS-DOS versions after 5.0. This will recreate the Master Boot Record of your hard drive. You'll only be able to boot to DOS after this command, but it can also fix a corrupted LILO setup.

If you do use LILO, be sure to have a floppy diskette handy just in case LILO gets corrupted or erased. When building your kernel, use the `make zdisk` command instead of `make zlilo`.

CHAPTER
11

- C Compiler—gcc and g++

- PERL—Practical Extraction and Reporting Language

- T_{CL}/T_K

Development Tools

I f you don't have the right tools available to suit your needs, the next option is to build your own. Fortunately, Linux comes with enough development tools to suit any level of programmer.

One of the best ways to see how a programming language works is through the use of a "hello" program. The only function of this program is to print the words "Hello world!" to the screen, then quit.

C Compiler—gcc and g++

The GNU C compiler is probably the most common development tool available for Linux, and is used to compile most of the kernel. In addition, gcc provides the libraries and header files needed to compile and run a majority of the programs that you use. The gcc manuals will help in figuring out what most of the options of the command itself are. C programs usually have an extension of .c, while a C++ program has an extension of .cc or .C. An object file (a compiled C file but one not ready to be executed) has an extension of .o. In short, to compile a C program is:

```
> gcc -o output output.c
```

The resulting program, called output, has the execute permission already set, so all you need to do to run your program is type

```
> ./output
```

Not here the use of the ./ in front of the program. To the shell, this means that the command you typed is located in the current directory and to only look in the current directory for that program. Assuming the program was compiled in /home/mark/programs, the line to the shell would look like this:

```
> /home/mark/programs/output
```

which you could type also, but ./ is much easier to remember. There are two reasons to run the program like this. First, in some secure setups, the current working directory is not in the path of some users. This means that even if you're in the same directory as the program, you can't run it. You'll get an output: Command not found error, which can be frustrating and confusing. The other reason is to make sure the shell runs the right copy of the program. For example, I had one user complain that the program he had just compiled did not work. He would type in the command, and the shell would immediately return without printing out any of the data he expected. As it turned out, he had named his program 'test.' If you look in /usr/bin, you'll find a program there called test which does exactly what the user saw: give no output and return to the shell. Once the user began executing. ./test, the correct copy of the test program executed and data was displayed.

A simple "hello world" program would look like this:

```
#include <stdio.h>
main() {
printf ("Hello world!\n");
}
```

PERL—Practical Extraction and Reporting Language

Perl has many of the advantages of a structured language like C, but is really an interpreted language. This gives the advantage of developing small programs quickly. In addition, editing can be performed quickly as the compiling of the script is done internally. Perl scripts (or they can be called programs) have a .pl extension.

The user writes up a perl script, and when the user wants to run the code, the perl program reads the script. The perl program then compiles the script internally and runs it. There are two ways to run a perl script:

1.   perl <filename>—This tells the perl program to use <filename> as a script. This can get rather tedious to type in after a while.

2.   <filename>—You have to do two thing to set this up. First, the execute permission must be set on the filename. Second, the first line of the perl script has to contain a line similar to this:

```
#!/usr/bin/perl
```

Replace the /usr/bin/perl with the location of the perl executable. Some systems don't include perl normally, so it may be located in /usr/local/bin/perl. Most Linux installations contain perl, so it will probably be located in /usr/bin/perl. This tells the shell what program to process the following script with. You may have seen some shell scripts that have something like this as the first line:

```
#!/bin/sh
```

and this is the same idea as perl.

Here's a hello world script written in perl:

```
#!/usr/bin/perl
print "Hello world!\n";
```

As you can see, this program is slightly smaller than the above C code. However, it does run a bit slower because each time this program is run, the perl program is also started. This adds overhead in terms of starting and in memory usage.

T_{CL}/T_K

The T_{CL}/T_K libraries are mainly for the X system. This allows for rapid prototyping (or production) of X programs. If you have ever written X programs in C, T_{CL} will seem very easy to use, as many of the low-level functions of creating a window and manipulating it are handled by the T_K widget kit. This leaves the programmer free to write the application instead of trying to remember how to open a window.

Programs in T_{CL}/T_K look similar to perl scripts in that a script is written and the interpreter (/usr/bin/wish or /usr/local/bin/wish) internally compiles the script.

Here's a sample T_{CL} program:

```
#!/usr/bin/wish -f
button .b -text "Hello world!" -command exit
pack .b
```

Comparing this to the more than thirty lines of C code needed to do the same thing in X, it is easy to see the power of T_{CL}/T_K:

```
/*      Just a silly little "Hello World" program for X. I'm actually using
 *      both the X-Intrinsics and the Athena Widget set to help. If I didn't,
 *      this could be many pages of code.
 *      build this using: cc xhello.c -o xhello -1Xt -1Xaw -1X11
 */

#include <X11/Intrinsic.h> /* We need headers from the X Intrinsics
#include <X11/StringDefs.h>   for the Xt function. */

#include <X11/Xaw/Label.h> /* And we need to borrow the label definition from
                              the Athena set. */

void main (int argc, char *argv[])
{
        Widget toplevel, text;
        XtAppContext app;

        /*Fairly simple, create the "main" window. */
        toplevel=XtAppInitialize(&app,"hello",NULL,0,&argc,argv,NULL,NULL,0);

        /*Create the text to go inside it. */
        text=XtVaCreateWidget("label",labelWidgetClass,toplevel,XtNlabel,
                        "Hello World!",NULL) ;

    /* Put the two widgets on the screen. */
    XtManageChild(text) ;
    XtRealizeWidget(toplevel) ;

    /* And go into an infinite loop . . . */
    XtAppMainLoop(app) ;
}
```

Even without the comments, the resulting C code is five times bigger than the T_{CL}/T_K code.

CHAPTER

12

- Security

- File Ownership

- Syslog

- Netiquette

- Recompiling a Kernel

System Administrator

Up until now, most of your UNIX experience has probably been as a user. If you plan on running a Linux system from your home that rarely connects to the Internet or some other network, the amount of upkeep that you have is rather minimal. Once you connect to the Internet or to an already existing LAN, you'll have to make sure the machine is running properly. Traditionally, this is the job of a system administrator; to make sure the system is running smoothly on the network and can communicate with other machines.

Now it's your job. Don't worry. A properly configured Linux system is relatively hassle-free. Of the two machines I administer on the Internet, I spend perhaps two hours a week. The tasks I perform include backups, security checks, monitoring the kernel logs, making sure the users are connecting properly, and so on.

Security

One of the most important jobs is security. This is making your Linux machine impervious to attacks.

These attacks can be an organized effort. Crackers may try to break into the root account. An attack could also be a simple case of programmer error when a machine on the network goes awry and begins overflowing the mail spool.

First let's discuss organized attacks. There are a lot of easy ways to increase the security of your machine against outside attackers and many of these ways deal with user training.

For example, user passwords should *never* be easy to guess. The idea behind a password is that a user will remember it, but only that person would know it.

Using a password such as a birthday, phone number, spouse's name, or favorite TV show are all bad choices. Here are some hints when choosing a password:

DO:

Use a mix of numbers and letters. Punctuation is also good.

Use a mix of upper and lowercase letters if possible.

Use abbreviations or portions of words put together.

Use more than four characters in the password.

Change your password often; once every few months is good, once every few weeks to be extra sure.

Tell the system administrator (you) if you suspect anyone else has used the account.

DO NOT:

Write a password down anywhere.

Tell anyone your password, especially over the phone or via e-mail. Use words you could find in a dictionary.

Use words that are easily guessable: proper nouns, repeated characters (AAAA), character patterns (abcdefg or qwerty).

Tell anyone the root password.

By following these guidelines, it will be harder for someone to break into your system.

File Ownership

The root account is the only account allowed to change the ownership of a file from one user to another. This is done through the `chown` command. The `chown` command will change the owner (and optionally, the group) of a file or group of files to another owner. If you give the `-R` command, the `chown` will recurse through directories. For example, the root user can change the ownership of a file to the user mark with the command

```
# chown mark file.txt
```

If you want to make sure the group is set to the users group, add a period and a group name after the user name. It would look something like this:

```
# chown mark.users file.txt
```

If you want to change only the group ownership of a file, you can use the `chgrp` command. Any user who is a member of more than one group can use `chgrp`.

```
> chgrp techcomm file.txt
```

Syslog

Another method of making your system more secure is to monitor what the system is doing. Using the syslogd daemon, the kernel and various daemons are all able to record events to a file to be reviewed later. For example, you could have syslog monitor all the attemts to log in by a username that does not exist.

Later, when these records are reviewed, they'll provide information that could help you track down whomever is trying to break into your system. Syslog is also extremely helpful in debugging many of the other daemons that Linux uses.

The syslogd daemon is typically started as part of the TCP/IP daemons located in /etc/rc.d/rc.inet2. If you do not have TCP/IP set up, syslog will get started by /etc/rc.d/rc.M. The reason that syslog uses TCP/IP is because it can send messages to other systems for monitoring. That is, a whole network of machines can send all of their logging information to one central machine so that problems can be quickly found and analyzed.

The configuration for syslog is located in the /etc/syslog.conf file. A sample syslog.conf file would look like this:

```
# /etc/syslog.conf
# For info about the format of this file, see "man syslog.conf" (the BSD man
# page), and /usr/doc/sysklogd/README.linux.
#
# NOTE: YOU HAVE TO USE TABS HERE - NOT SPACES.
# I don't know why.
#
*.info;*.notice                         /var/adm/messages
*.debug                                 /var/adm/debug
*.warn                                  /var/adm/syslog
#
# This might work instead to log on a remote host:
# *                     @hostname
```

As in most other configuration files, any line that has a pound sign (#) will be ignored from that character to the end of the line. The general setup of the file entries is of the form:

```
facility.level [; facility.level]       filename
```

There are ten standard facilities, plus eight locally defined ones. The facilities are listed here:

user—Default facility; usually sent by user programs

kern—Kernel messages

mail—Mail system; provides messages about where mail came from, when mail was sent daemon—Various daemons (ftpd, etc)

auth—Handles user accounts, such as login, su, getty: can track who logs in, when someone fails to log in, and when someone fails (or succeeds) at attaining root account status through su

lpr—Line printer daemon

news—USENET news system

uucp—Unix-to-Unix copy system

cron—Programs like cron and at

mark—Special facility that gets triggered internally by syslogd every twenty minutes or so

*—Special facility that means all facilities except mark.

The locally defined facilities are local0 through local7. These can be used by user programs, or by the logger program.

Each facility should also have a severity level associated with it. Using this, simple debugging messages can get sent to one file while more serious errors get sent to another file (or another machine).

There are a total of nine severity levels available:

emerg—A panic condition that would usually broadcast a message to all users

alert—A condition that should be corrected immediately, such as a corrupted database

crit—Warnings about critical conditions, such as a hard drive error

err—Other errors

warning—Other warnings

notice—A condition that is not an error, but may need special handling

info—Informational messages

debug—Debugging information (this will cause a lot of output)

none—Do not send messages from the selected facility to the file.

The third option specifies where to send the logged information to. If the option begins with a forward slash (/), then syslogd will write the information to that file. If the option is a hostname and starts with an @, then syslog will try and transmit the messages to that host. If the option has a list of users separated by a comma, then the users in that list will receive the message on their screen if they're logged in. If the option is a star (*), then all users who are logged on will receive the message.

For example, if I wanted all of the emerg information to go to all of the users who are logged in, I could have an entry like this:

```
*.emerg                    *
```

Whereas if I wanted alert information to be sent to my screen, and get logged in a file, I'd need two entries. One would be to send the message to my screen, and the other to send the message to the file:

```
*.alert                 mfk
*.alert                 /var/adm/syslog.alert
```

You'll see that the file here and the files in the above example both use the /var/adm directory. This is where most files of this nature should go. To keep things straight, you may want to name your files based on what they do. For example, alert messages would go in syslog.alert, while err messages go into syslog.err. This makes for easy tracking of the severity of messages. If you see the time and date stamp of the file change, this means a message was written to it.

Now you're probably wondering what the none severity is used for, especially if it tells syslog *not* to log something. The none level can be used to remove a particular facility. For example, if I wanted to log the alert messages from every facility but the user facility, I could have an entry like this:

```
*.alert;user.none       /var/adm/syslog.nouser.alert
```

Netiquette

Having access to the root account not only gives you great power, but great responsibility as well. This is especially true if you plan on providing user accounts to others. Given the scope of the abilities that the root account has, it is very easy to misuse them.

Here are some guidelines on how to handle users. Most of them are common sense, but they're very important to remember.

1. Don't read other peoples' files.

2. Don't read other users' mail.

3. If someone else is logged in, provide some time for the user to complete their programs before rebooting the machine. Unless it's an absolute emergency, you can schedule reboots through the shutdown command. Then you can send messages to all users when the command is run, at ten minutes before shutdown, five minutes before shutdown, and one minute before shutdown.

4. Don't delete programs without checking if it's really needed or not. Just because you don't use the vi editor doesn't mean that it's an unneeded program.

5. Keep up-to-date with bug fixes and security alerts. If someone breaks into your system, your users will come after you first.

6. Don't assume the status of another user through su.

7. Don't ask for information about a user's password

8.   Tell users what's going on. You'll minimize the number of calls or e-mail messages you get if you provide information about recent problems. One file to look at is the `/etc/motd` file. This file is displayed to most users when they log in. Spending thirty seconds to edit this file to explain why the phone lines were down can cut the number of calls you get from users.

Recompiling a Kernel

While some changes to your Linux system may not require you to recompile your kernel, there are instances where doing it is necessary. Such examples include:

New version of the kernel

Adding or changing SCSI support

Adding or changing network cards

Adding parallel printer support

Sound card setup

Let's take the case where you want to add a new version of the kernel. Once you actually get a new kernel, the rest is rather easy. You can get a new kernel via FTP from sunsite.unc.edu or nic.funet.fi. Once you have the new kernel on your Linux system, copy it to the `/usr/src` directory as root. Next, backup the previous kernel source. This way, you can go back to an older release rather easily. If you're upgrading from kernel version 1.2.8 to a newer kernel, you could do this:

```
# mv linux linux-1.2.8
```

This is the easiest way to remember what version is in the directory. Next, uncompress and untar the Linux source code. If you're uncompressing Linux version 1.2.13, you'll have a command similar to this:

```
# tar -zxvf linux-1.2.13.tar.gz
```

or

```
# gunzip -c linux-1.2.13 | tar -xvf -
```

The two commands will do the same thing, but some versions of tar may not allow you to use the `-z` switch. Use the second command if this is the case.

This will create a directory called `linux` which contains the source code for the kernel. Enter the linux directory and type

```
# make config
```

This is the way that you configure the compile-time options for the kernel. This is where you select SCSI support, network cards, and so on.

If you don't know the answer to a particular question, it is usually safe to take the default. There are a few important things to note:

Filesystem support. Be sure you add support for the type of filesystem you are using Linux from. In most cases, this is ext2fs. If you're using UMSDOS, be sure to include that. If you have a CD-ROM and plan on using it, be sure to add support for ISO9660. And also be sure to include support for the `/proc` filesystem.

SCSI support. If you don't have a SCSI card, it is safe to answer 'no' to this. If you have a SCSI CD-ROM, then select 'yes' and be sure to select SCSI CD-ROM support and choose the particular SCSI card you are using.

CD-ROM support. This is only for proprietary interfaces. If you have a SCSI or IDE (ATAPI) CD-ROM, it will automatically be supported in the SCSI or IDE sections.

Once you have the kernel configured, type

```
# make dep
```

This does some setup for the files that need to be compiled. Once this is completed, you have your choice of building the kernel. You can either make the kernel and not install it (not very useful), or you can make and install the kernel to a floppy disk or to the LILO program.

If you install the kernel to a floppy disk, you'll need that diskette in the boot disk (usually /dev/fd0 or A:) when the machine starts for that kernel to load. Put a floppy disk in the drive and type

```
# make zdisk
```

Once the kernel compile is completed, it will put the kernel on the floppy. The 'zdisk' means that the kernel will automatically be compressed so that it takes up about a third of the space of an uncompressed kernel. This allows the kernel to fit on floppy disks if you enable a lot of options. My kernel size is just under 1MB uncompressed, but takes up about 350k compressed. As Linux starts to boot, it uncompresses the kernel to memory.

If you use LILO to boot your machine, you can have the new kernel automatically added to the LILO setup so that the new kernel will boot the next time you boot the machine. Make sure that LILO is already installed on your machine before doing this, then type

```
# make zlilo
```

The kernel for LILO is also compressed, and can be found in the root directory as `vmlinuz`. The z at the end of the filename means the file is compressed.

If you type make by itself, this will build the kernel and leave it in `/usr/src/linux`. Once the kernel finishes its build and you don't see the `vmlinux` file, you can find it by typing

```
# find /usr/src/linux -name "vmlinux"
```

The location of the `vmlinux` file may change as Linux supports more platforms.

CHAPTER
13

- Configuring Logins

- Deleting Accounts

Handling Users

For most installations, the passwords and other user account information is stored in the /etc/passwd file. There are only two big cases where this is not quite true. First, if you're using shadow passwords, some of the account information is stored in /etc/shadow. This file is readable only by root. Another case is if you're using a distributed user system such as Kerberos. Kerberos allows a user to securely log into a remote host through a network.

A typical line in /etc/passwd looks like this:

```
mfk:SsuF75wj/cZqs:405:100:Mark Komarinski:/home/mfk:/bin/tcsh
```

Adding a new user to the system can be done by merely adding an entry in the /etc/passwd file for the user. You can see that there are seven fields here. The first is the username consisting of eight lowercase characters or numbers. The second field (that large jumble of letters and numbers) is the encrypted password. The password is encrypted such that it is very hard to decrypt. In fact, when you enter a password upon login, the login program encrypts the password you enter and compares the encrypted text with the entry in /etc/passwd. If the two strings match, you are allowed into the system.

The third field is the UID, which should be (but not necessarily) a unique number less than 65535 and greater than 0. The fourth field is the GID, and relates to an entry in /etc/group. In this case, GID 100 relates to the group called users. If you examined the /etc/group file, you'd find an entry like this:

```
users::100:games
```

The GID represents the primary group that the user is in.

The next field gives personal information about the user, such as a full name, office location, phone numbers, and so on. This is one of the fields that can be

125

changed by the user without the help of the root account. The `chfn` command allows the user to change this personal information.

The sixth field (`/home/mfk`) is the location of the home directory. This is important to know because the various shell startup files such as .login, .profile, or .cshrc are there. This directory should be owned by the user, and should have write, read, and execute permissions for the user only.

The last field refers to the shell that is run when the user logs in. You should note that you can have any program in here as long as the program is also listed in `/etc/shells`.

A default `/etc/shells` file has the following entries:

```
/bin/sh
/bin/bash
/bin/tcsh
/bin/csh
```

If a program is entered in the seventh field of the `/etc/passwd` entry, but the program is not entered in `/etc/shell`, the user will not be able to log in.

If you want to add a new shell, say the public domain ksh implementation, you must compile the pdksh and install it in `/bin`. After this, log in to the root account and add an entry for pdksh like this:

```
/bin/pdksh
```

Once this entry is made and the file is saved, any user should be able to use the `chsh` command to change their default shell to be `/bin/pdksh`.

```
linux:~> chsh

Enter password:

The current shell is: /bin/tcsh

You can choose one of the following:

1: /bin/sh
2: /bin/bash
3: /bin/tcsh
4: /bin/csh
5: /bin/pdksh
Enter a number between 1 and 5: 5
Shell changed.
linux:~>
```

Without the entry in `/etc/shells`, the `/bin/pdksh` entry would not be listed as an option. In addition, if you were to manually edit `/etc/passwd` to make the shell `/bin/pdksh` without the entry in `/etc/shells`, you would not be able to log in.

Some installations contain a program called /sbin/adduser which interactively creates a user for you. You provide a username, GID, home directory, and other information to adduser. It then creates the entry in /etc/passwd, creates the home directory, copies some startup files into that directory, then sets proper ownership and permissions for that home directory. Once that command is complete, the user account is set up.

Configuring Logins

When you use the adduser command to create a new account, it will copy the files that exist in the /etc/skel directory into the new account home. My directory looks like this:

```
drwxr-xr-x     3    root    root    1024    Jan 16   1995    .
drwxr-xr-x    11    root    root    4096    Sep  5 12:58    ..
-rw-------     1    root    root       9    Feb 15   1994    .bashrc
-rw-r--r--     1    root    root    3016    May 13   1994    .emacs
-rw-r--r--     1    root    root     163    Nov 23   1993    .kermrc
-rw-r--r--     1    root    root      34    Jun  6   1993    .less
-rw-r--r--     1    root    root     114    Nov 23   1993    .lessrc
drwxr-xr-x     2    root    root    1024    Jan 16   1995    .term
-rwx--x--x     1    root    root     944    Feb 15   1994    .xinitrc
```

The .term directory has a file called termrc. If you add more files to this directory, they will be added to each new account you add.

The way that your account starts up depends on the shell you use. If you use the /bin/csh shell, this will be the .cshrc file. The bash shell uses .profile, and other shells can use these files or additional ones. For example, the /bin/tcsh shell has a .tcshrc file that reads in additional data that is used only by tcsh. This keeps extra commands out of .cshrc in case you switch back.

The first thing you should do is choose a login shell. This can be any of the standard shells such as csh (/bin/tcsh) or sh (/bin/bash) or can be any of the other shells that exist, such as pdksh or zsh. You may want to think about a few things, however.

The sh shell is usually the best for programming shell scripts, but the worst at user interface. The /bin/bash shell makes up for much of this, however. Functions such as command-line editing and interactive histories are supported.

The csh shell is usually better at the user interface, but has little scripting. I find the interface and functionality of the csh shell is best, so I'll use that for our example.

If you use the -a switch to ls, you can get a list of the 'dot' files that exist in your home directory. They're called dot files because the files start with a period (or a dot). You may or may not find a file called either .cshrc or .tcshrc. If you find either, you can examine it and see how the file is setup. If you don't have the file, that's ok. If you want another template file to work from, look in the /etc directory. For example, there's the /etc/csh.cshrc and /etc/csh.login files.

The .login file is run when the user logs in. It contains information about logging in, such as setting the terminal type.

The .cshrc file or the .profile (.profile is used by bash) is used each time a new instance of csh or bash gets started. The difference? A login shell is used once, when you log in. A .cshrc file is run each time an instance of the shell is started.

If you log into your Linux machine and you're using the tcsh, both the .login and .cshrc get run by the shell. If you start a program such as the vi editor, then shell out (using the ! command), only the .cshrc gets executed.

You should remember that when you shell out of a program, the setup you see will not be exactly the same as when you originally logged in. This is true not only for shelling out of programs, but when you start the X-Window System as well.

There is one advantage to the .login setup. In some instances you'll want a program or series of programs to run each time you log in. For example, I have two extra programs run upon login. One checks my mail to tell me if I have new mail or not, and another (fortune) provides a quote for the day. Since I don't want these programs run each time I start a shell, I include the calls to these programs in my .login. Other functions are in my .cshrc file.

You can check the default setups by looking in the /etc/csh.login and /etc/csh.cshrc files. There is also the /etc/profile file used by bash.

Deleting Accounts

Deleting an account really depends on why you want to remove the account. If you want the user to never log in again, simply delete the line entry in /etc/profile using your favorite editor. The files from the user can be removed by deleting the home directory of the user.

If you want to deactivate the account for some amount of time (say the user is going on a vacation and you don't want anyone using the account) you can deactivate the account. Deactivating the account can be done in more than one way. The easiest is to place an asterisk (*) in front of the password field of /etc/passwd. This makes the password practically uncrackable, since the asterisk is not part of the password at all. When login tries to match an entered password with the one stored in /etc/passwd, they won't match. Once the user returns, you can edit the `passwd` file again and remove the asterisk, leaving the original password intact.

Since this can be confusing, there is an easier method of deactivating an account for a period of time. Create a shell script that looks something like this:

```
#!/bin/sh
trap 0 1 2 3 5 9
echo "This account has been deactivated.\n"
echo "Please see the system administrator for more information.\n"
exit
```

Call it something like `/bin/deactive`, add it to `/etc/shells`, and make it the login shell for the user. While the password will work, the following will happen when the user successfully logs in:

```
Welcome to Linux 1.2.13.

trippy login: mark

password:

This account has been deactivated.

Please see the system administrator for more information.

Welcome to Linux 1.2.13.

trippy login:
```

They're able to enter the correct user name and password, but the default shell (/bin/deactive) informs the user that the account was deactivated, then logs them out.

When you want to reactivate the account, simply replace the `/bin/deactive` with some other login shell, such as `/bin/tcsh`.

There are a few things to remember about removing accounts. Removing the account from `/etc/passwd` does not mean that all of that user's files are deleted. The files will still exist, and have an ownership of the UID of the old file. Say we remove the gonzo account (which has a UID of 408). If you get a directory of the gonzo home directory, you'll see somethine like this:

```
> ls -la ~gonzo
total 12
drwxr-xr-x    3    gonzo    users    1024    Mar  9  1995   .
drwxr-xr-x   15    root     root     1024    May  4 18:22   ..
-rw-r--r--    1    gonzo    users       5    Mar  9  1995   .bash_history
-rw-------    1    gonzo    users       9    Mar  9  1995   .bashrc
-rw-r--r--    1    gonzo    users    3016    Mar  9  1995   .emacs
-rw-r--r--    1    gonzo    users     163    Mar  9  1995   .kermrc
-rw-r--r--    1    gonzo    users      34    Mar  9  1995   .less
-rw-r--r--    1    gonzo    users     114    Mar  9  1995   .lessrc
```

```
drwxr-xr-x    2     gonzo     users     1024  Mar  9  1995  .term
-rwx--x--x    1     gonzo     users      944  Mar  9  1995  .xinitrc
>
```

When the account is removed from /etc/passwd, and you try another directory of gonzo's home directory, here's what will happen:

```
> ls -la ~gonzo
Unknown user: gonzo.
>
```

This was rather easy to predict, since the account no longer exists. Since you remember that the home directory was /home/gonzo, let's check that directory:

```
> ls -la /home/gonzo
total 12
drwxr-xr-x    3   408      users     1024  Mar  9   1995  .
drwxr-xr-x   15   root     root      1024  May  4  18:22  ..
-rw-r--r--    1   408      users        5  Mar  9   1995  .bash_history
-rw-------    1   408      users        9  Mar  9   1995  .bashrc
-rw-r--r--    1   408      users     3016  Mar  9   1995  .emacs
-rw-r--r--    1   408      users      163  Mar  9   1995  .kermrc
-rw-r--r--    1   408      users       34  Mar  9   1995  .less
-rw-r--r--    1   408      users      114  Mar  9   1995  .lessrc
drwxr-xr-x    2   408      users     1024  Mar  9   1995  .term
-rwx--x--x    1   408      users      944  Mar  9   1995  .xinitrc >
```

Sure enough, the user name is gone from the files. The files still exist, and the owner is UID 408. If you create a new account with the name fred and it gets UID 408, then the above files will be owned by the fred account.

The problems with this are somewhat obvious. When the new user gets created, the new user may get ownership of these files. In most cases, this is more of an annoyance than anything else. The new user discovers files all over the place that he or she never created. In some cases, these new files could have security holes in them. The best thing do do, of course, would be to remove (or back up) all the files of the old user before creating a new user.

Here you can use the find command to find all the files of that user. There are two ways you can use the find command. You can simply locate all the files and know where they are, or find the files and remove all of them.

To find all the files, run this command:

```
> find / -user gonzo -print
```

This will simply list the files owned by the gonzo user. If you want to remove the files, add the -exec command to the find command:

```
> find / -user gonzo -print -exec rm \{\} \;
```

While it looks a bit more complicated than the above example, not only does this list the files that gonzo owns, but it also removes them. You can replace the rm \{\} with anything else, such as a mv \{\} /tmp/backup/gonzo. This would move all the files owned by gonzo into the /tmp/backup/gonzo directory. From there, you could back it up to a tape or just delete the files.

CHAPTER 14

- Serial Printers

- Modifying Parallel Printer Support

- Modems and Multiport Cards

- External Terminal

- Sound Cards

Printer and Other Device Support

The first thing that you have to make sure of when adding a printer to a Linux system is that there is printer support in the kernel. To do this, go through a `make config` until you see the section on CONFIG_PRINTER. Set this to 'yes' and continue with the configuration. Make the kernel and reboot with the new kernel. Make sure that the normal printer IRQ (7) isn't being used by another device, such as the sound card. There are ways to let the parallel port use another IRQ, or to set the printer port to 'polling' mode.

If your printer is on the first parallel port, you can enter this command as root to make sure the printer software and the connections are working properly:

```
# ls > /dev/lp0
```

If your printer is on the second parallel port, change the redirect to be `/dev/lp1` or `/dev/lp2` if the printer is on the third parallel port.

If a directory listing comes out, then the connection is working properly and you can go on. Don't worry if your output has a staircase effect like this:

```
INDEX.whole              imagemap*              netpbm/
                                                      INDEX.whole.gz

          kguide-0.2.tgz             new-3.gif
                                           NEW                 kguide.RE
ADME               new.gif
```

The reason for this is that Linux and the printer don't agree (yet) on what character or characters should be at the end of the line. This can be fixed later on. The important part (that the printer and Linux communicate) works.

The program used in Linux to handle print jobs and actually interact with the printers is called lpd, for line printer daemon. In many respects, the lpd program is similar to Window's Print Manager program. Print jobs can be listed, added, or deleted. Print jobs can also be sent to local or remote printers via the network.

The file used to configure lpd is called `/etc/printcap`. This file has entries in it to relate to each printer you want to set up. The lpd program has the ability to have multiple printer setups for the same physical printer.

If you look in the `/etc/printcap` file, you can see how the various printers are setup. Each line starting with a # is a comment. You will probably see one entry that is not commented out, being the Generic Printer setup. It probably looks something like this:

```
# Generic printer:
lp:lp=/dev/lp1:sd=/usr/spool/lp1:sh
```

If this entry is commented out with a # in front of it, remove the #. Also change the `/dev/lp1` if you're using `/dev/lp2` or `/dev/lp0`.

Now, go to a shell prompt and see if lpd is running already:

```
> ps -aux | grep lpd
mfk   2392    0.0   1.3   153   204   pp0   S   11:26   0:00   grep lpd
root    53    0.0   1.3    64   204   con   S   Sep 5   0:00   /usr/sbin/lpd >
```

In most setups with TCP/IP installed, lpd is started automatically. If lpd isn't running, start lpd from the root account. You can also add a line in the `/etc/rc.d/rc.local` file to start the lpd each time Linux boots.

Now, test lpd with the following:

```
> ls | lpr -Plp
```

The lpr program is the user program that sends jobs to lpd. The -Plp switch tells lpr which print queue to enter the job into. In our example, we use the lp printer, since that is the entry in the `/etc/printcap` file. Now you should see the output on your printer. This will probably look the same as your earlier test.

For most users, this should do it. If you have a dot-matrix printer and have the staircase effect, there may be a DIP switch in the printer to change the End Of Line (or EOL) characters from CRLF to CR. For users with laser printers that have the staircase effect, there are programs available to send the correct codes to the printer.

Some printers will be able to use a program called 'magicfilter' which allows you to print many different kinds of files all directly to your printer. For example, you could send a raw postscript file to your dot-matrix printer. The magicfilter program converts the postscript file to a format your printer can understand automatically. You can find magicfilter at most of the major Linux FTP sites listed in Appendix A.

Serial Printers

Users with serial printers can change the entry in /etc/printcap so that the lp= points to the correct output device (lp=/dev/cua1). Also add the 'br' entry which specifies the baud rate. (br#1200 for 1200 baud).

You can test your serial port with a command similar to this:

```
> (stty 9600 ; ls -la ) > /dev/cua1
```

Note that you may get the staircase effect mentioned above. Once you get the printer set up or install a program like magicfilter, the staircase effect should end.

You should be sure of the speed of the serial printer before you begin. Most printers have a way of setting this or finding it out. You should also be sure the serial printer has a null modem connection on it. If the printer works fine in another operating system, you won't need to worry about the null modem connector. More information about how the printcap file works and its entries can be found in the printcap manual page.

Modifying Parallel Printer Support

The tunelp program will allow you to use another IRQ for the parallel port if your hardware allows it. Another option is to use polling mode, where Linux does not use IRQs at all. Polling is less efficient, since the CPU has to work harder to communicate with the parallel port. But if you're stuck and need a free IRQ, the benefits may outweigh the disadvantages.

Modems and Multiport Cards

If your modem is already installed in the machine, there is no need to reboot the Linux system to use the modem or multiport card. If your modem is not installed, follow the modem instructions to install it. Be sure to remember the COM port setting.

You should know how the serial ports are accessed in Linux. There are two different names to access each serial device. COM1 in DOS or Windows is known to Linux as both /dev/ttyS0 and /dev/cua0. The /dev/ttyS is for incoming data, and /dev/cua is for outgoing data. This allows you to have a program waiting on the serial port for an incoming call (so that you can dial into the machine) while you use the modem to dial out to another machine. In effect, two programs are watching the same serial port, while only one can control it at one time.

A program called 'setserial' is available which sets up the kernel for the type of modem you have. Fortunately, many Linux installations have a program located in /etc/rc.d called rc.serial which will automatically set most modems.

This information has to be set because the kernel needs to know what kind of UART chips your serial ports use. UART chips are used to actually transmit the data through a serial line, and there are many kinds of UARTS. Systems with modems faster than 14.4k should use the rc.serial script when booting Linux. The rc.serial script calls setserial for all the standard serial ports (/dev/ttyS0 through /dev/ttyS3) and has commands for finding and activating some multi-port cards.

If you have a multiport serial card that is supported under Linux, you can use the rc.serial script to activate the cards as well. Find the section of the script that refers to the board you installed (such as the AST Fourport, BocaBoard, and so on) and remove the # characters in front of the lines. If you have a board that is not listed, but you know that Linux supports it, contact the manufacturer for installation instructions.

One other advantage to setserial is that it can tell the Linux kernel where non-standard serial ports are. To understand this, you have to look at how the PC architecture assigns serial ports. By default, there are four serial ports. COM1 and COM3 are on IRQ 4, while COM2 and COM4 are on IRQ 3. The reason for this is that DOS could only do one thing at a time, and it was able to share IRQs. Now that Linux is around, it's harder to share these IRQs, since one program may be using /dev/ttyS1, while another program is trying to access /dev/ttyS3. This would cause an IRQ conflict that could cause all serial ports to malfunction.

As a result, some modems or serial port cards allow you to use another IRQ for a specified COM port. To tell Linux of the change, the setserial program will do this for you. The call to setserial would look something like this:

```
# setserial -b /dev/cua0 irq 15 autoconfig
```

if you had COM1 set to IRQ 15. You can change it to fit your particular situation. Look at the man pages for setserial and also look at /etc/rc.d/rc.serial for some setups.

Some video cards or other IO cards (such as the Mach32 card) use the same IO locations as the third or fourth serial port. If the text on your screen changes after rc.serial or setserial runs, check the user manual for your video card. Otherwise, make sure that only the serial ports you are using are uncommented. Comment out other setserial commands by putting a # character as the first character of the line.

Once the modem is set up, you can use a program like minicom, seyon, or kermit to dial into other computers. You can also start up a PPP or SLIP link. The next chapter gets into networking.

External Terminal

Another option is hooking up a dumb terminal or another PC to the serial port. This allows multiple people to connect to the Linux machine without using networking software. The advantages of this is that it's cheap and easy to do, because you don't need network cables or network cards for the communication, nor do you have to configure the software all that much. The disadvantages are that for the most part, you won't have all the networking capabilities. You cannot, for example, share hard drive space or display X programs remotely. The best you will get is a dumb terminal, with text only. But it's a good use for the old 80286 machine you have collecting dust in the basement. Make it a remote terminal! Let the kids play rogue or nethack while you read USENET or use the World Wide Web.

To do this, however, you'll need some hardware. First, you need a terminal that will accept a serial port input. If you know a nearby computer person who has a few spare VT220 terminals, those work perfectly. Or if you have a spare 80286 or a mac, or any other kind of machine, that will work. Next you'll need what's known as a null modem cable. Because of the way that a serial cable operates, two of the wires have to be flipped. You can usually find a null modem connector or even a cable with the null modem built in at an electronics store or at a computer fair.

After connecting the null modem cable between the Linux machine and your other PC, make a note of the serial port you're going to use and the speed you want to use. For the most part, you can get away with an 8-bit, no parity, 1-stop bit connection at a speed of about 9600 bps. If you feel daring, you can try to boost this speed up some. If the speed gets too high, the connection won't work and you'll need to drop it down some. The best speed I have gotten is about 19.2k bps.

Now you'll need to edit the `/etc/inittab` file. So su to the root account and fire up your favorite editor. Most implementations of `/etc/inittab` already have some setups for dumb terminals. You may see a group of lines like this:

```
# Serial lines
#s1:45:respawn:/sbin/agetty 9600 ttyS0
#s2:45:respawn:/sbin/agetty 9600 ttyS1
```

If so, just uncomment the one you want to use (or change it if you're using an-other serial port). Going back to our discussion of how init works, this will start on runlevels of 4 or 5. Assuming that we started in runlevel 5, this will automatically start up next time we reboot. But if you want to start it immediately, you can use the telinit program to manually switch to runlevel 5 and start the agetty program.

```
# telinit 5
```

After this command finishes, a `ps -aux` will show:

```
root 348 5.0 1.2 41 192 pS1 S 22:01 0:00 /sbin/agetty 9600 tty
```

or something like

```
root 348 5.0 1.2 41 192 pS1 S 22:01 0:00 /bin/login Welcome to
```

From the other side, you should be able to start up a communication program, set the speed to 9600 bps, no parity, 8-bit, 1-stop bit, and you should be rewarded (perhaps after hitting 'Enter' a few times) with

```
Welcome to Linux
login:
```

For more help in connecting external terminals and a diagram for making your own null modem cables, check the most recent Serial-HOWTO.

Sound Cards

Most of the major sound cards are supported under Linux. The support is currently built into the kernel, but some future kernels will allow you to load the sound card support in modules.

Due to the way sound cards work, you usually have to know more about the sound card than the other hardware. If these settings are not correct, it can be quite a hassle to recompile the kernel and restart the system to load in the correct values.

Once the kernel is successfully installed, you'll need the software to use the sound card. There are numerous programs available for playing .wav, .au, and other formats of digital audio and music. The simplest way of using your sound card is to capture data from the 'in' or 'line' port of the sound card:

```
# cat /dev/audio > file.au
```

This will import data from the sound card in the .au format at 8khz to the specified file. To play the data back, you can have a command similar to

```
# cat file.au > /dev/audio
```

There are other device files available:

```
/dev/midi - Handles MIDI (Musical XXXX Digital Interface) data
/dev/sequencer - For FM synthesized data
/dev/audio - Digital sound (line in and line out)
/dev/dsp - Digital signal processor
```

Using these accurately requires the use of programs such as wavplay, sox, au-play, and other assorted programs available from most FTP sites.

CHAPTER
15

- Ifconfig

- Route

- Dialup

- PPP/SLIP Setups

Networking

The primary method for Linux to communicate to other Linux or UNIX machines is through TCP/IP. Besides TCP/IP, Linux supports protocols like IPX, AppleTalk, and LanMan. This chapter will cover TCP/IP since it is the most widely used protocol on the Internet.

Telnet, FTP, e-mail, and the World Wide Web all rely on TCP/IP communication to send data back and forth. In order for all of this to work, both machines (the client and server) need to have TCP/IP set up.

Most of the details in setting up the software is telling the kernel a few crucial facts:

1. Our IP address
2. The main gateway IP address (there may be more than one)
3. Netmask (there may be more than one of these as well)
4. Broadcast address (optional)
5. Network address

If you're adding this to an existing network, talk to your network administrator about these values. You can't just arbitrarily assign values. If you're using a dialup protocol like SLIP or PPP, much of this is handled by the software that opens the connection. You can safely ignore the following on ifconfig and route.

If you have a small-scale network that is not connected to the Internet, such as two or three machines networked together, you can assign whatever IP addresses you want. But let's first look at how networks are set up.

In order for one machine to communicate to another, the sending machine has to know what the other IP address is and it has to know how to send the data packets to that other machine.

In a small network, this is rather easy, as the Ethernet protocol (on a lower level than TCP/IP) allows two machines to see each other. All you need is the IP address of the other machine.

In a much larger network (such as the Internet) there have to be ways to tell a data packet how to get to another network. The gateway is used to forward a data packet to another network if the remote machine isn't on the local network. It acts as a bridge between two different local area networks. The netmask is used to tell what packets should get sent to the gateway, and what should be sent out on the local Ethernet to be received.

An IP address is a 32-bit number broken up into four groups of eight bits. Each group is called an octet. That means that the valid range of IP addresses runs from 0.0.0.0 through 255.255.255.255. This gives a theoretical limit of about 4.2 billion IP addresses available for use. In order to create logical networks out of these 4 billion addresses, they are grouped into 4 classes of networks. These networks can then be subnetworked (or subnetted).

These four classes are listed here:

Class A: 0.0.0.0 through 127.255.255.255

Class B: 128.0.0.0 through 191.255.255.255

Class C: 192.0.0.0 through 223.255.255.255

Reserved addresses: 234.0.0.0 through 255.255.255.255

Some of these classes (such as Class C) then follow a hierarchy much like the physical connection to a desk would look.

BigCommCorp has IP address 192.0.0.0 through 192.255.255.255. It then portions off the address range 192.5.0.0 through 192.5.255.255 to LittleCommCorp. LittleCommCorp then portions off 192.5.10.0 through 192.5.10.255 to your business. Don't actually try using these numbers on the Internet, this is just an example.

Looking back up the hierarchy, this means that your company has a total of 256 IP addresses that it can assign. LittleCommCorp has 65536 IP addresses assigned to it, or 256 groups of 256 IP addresses. BigCommCorp then has 256 groups of 256 subgroups of 256 IP addresses, for a total of about 16 million IP addresses. The total number is actually smaller than that, because some IP addresses (such as 255 and 0) are reserved.

An address ending in 255 is often used as a broadcast address. Any TCP/IP packet that gets sent out ending in 255 is received by all computers on that network. The 0 IP address is often used to define a network. That is, our network would be 192.5.10.0.

There is more than one way to break down a network. For example, you could have two subnets, one that went from 192.5.10.0 through 192.5.10.127 and the other from 192.5.10.128 through 192.5.10.255. To tell your machine how your network is subgrouped, you need the netmask. It sets how big your network is, when to go to your gateway, or when to look locally.

Once you have this information, use the ifconfig and route programs to tell the kernel about your network setups. Let's create a fake network setup based on the above IP setup:

Your IP address: 192.5.10.30

Netmask: 192.5.10.0

Gateway: 192.5.10.20

Broadcast: 192.5.10.255

Network Address: 192.5.10.0

Ifconfig

The ifconfig program will show or modify the network interfaces. The primary Ethernet interface is /dev/eth0, or just eth0 when you access it through ifconfig. The second ethernet device is eth1, and so on. Running ifconfig without any options will show the network setup as it is when you started Linux. There is one default route that is set up if you use the loopback device. Every TCP/IP machine has one special IP address that it uses to refer to itself: 127.0.0.1. No matter what IP address your machine has, any access to 127.0.0.1 will go to itself. The loopback device is needed to use the X-Windowing System and programs like syslogd. If you have the loopback device installed, you can see its setup:

```
>/sbin/ifconfig
        Link encap Local Loopback
        inet addr 127.0.0.1 Bcast 127.255.255.255 Mask 255.0.0.0
        UP BROADCAST LOOPBACK RUNNING MTU 2000 Metric 1
        RX packets 0 errors 0 dropped 0 overruns 0
        TX packets 0 errors 0 dropped 0 overruns 0
>
```

If you do not have a loopback device setup, you can start it with the following commands:

```
#/sbin/ifconfig lo 127.0.0.1
#/sbin/route add -net 127.0.0.0
```

The `lo` device here refers to the loopback. `eth0` refers to the Ethernet device, and `ppp` refers to the ppp interface.

You can now start adding interfaces. Looking at the man-page for ifconfig, you'll see all of the options it accepts. Here are a few of the major ones:

```
ifconfig [interface] address [options]
```

Options:

up—Bring the interface up for sending and receiving packets.

down—Take the interface down. Packets will not get sent or received. Good way to take your machine off the network if there are problems.

netmask addr—Netmask address

broadcast [addr]—sets the broadcast address

addresa—IP address (or a host name)

In some cases the placement of the options are significant in that the difference between a working interface and a nonworking one can be as simple as listing the netmask before the broadcast. If you have an /etc/rc.d/rc.inet1 file, you'll probably see the following lines:

```
# Uncomment ONLY ONE of the three lines below. If one doesn't work, try again.
# /sbin/ifconfig eth0 ${IPADDR} netmask ${NETMASK} broadcast ${BROADCAST}
# /sbin/ifconfig eth0 ${IPADDR} broadcast ${BROADCAST} netmask ${NETMASK}
# /sbin/ifconfig eth0 ${IPADDR} netmask ${NETMASK}
```

So we'll add a line to the `rc.inet1` file such that it looks something like this:

```
/sbin/ifconfig eth0 192.5.10.30 netmask 192.5.10.0 broadcast 192.5.10.255
```

Once the interface is up, you now have to tell the kernel how to route packets. Let's look at the output from the ifconfig again:

```
>/sbin/ifconfig
lo          Link encap Local Loopback
            inet addr 127.0.0.1 Bcast 127.255.255.255 Mask 255.0.0.0
            UP BROADCAST LOOPBACK RUNNING MTU 2000 Metric 1
            RX packets 0 errors 0 dropped 0 overruns 0
            TX packets 0 errors 0 dropped 0 overruns 0

>
```

This displays much of the data to tell you how the link is working. For example, the second line of text shows the IP address, broadcast, and the netmask. The third line shows the various flags that are associated with the link; in this case, the link is up, it's broadcasting, and it's a loopback device (as opposed to a point-to-point or Ethernet). The MTU is the maximum transmission unit, the biggest block of data that can be sent in one TCP/IP packet. For Ethernet or loopback devices, the MTU can be large, such as 2000 bytes. The upcoming section on SLIP and PPP connections will cover MTUs for dialup devices.

The fourth and fifth lines show transmission stats for the link. The fourth line shows the numbers of packets sent, the number of packets that didn't make it (had an error in the packet) the number of dropped packets, and the number of overruns. Looking at the number of error, dropped, or overrun packets can tell you if there's a problem in your Ethernet cable (if there are a lot of overruns) or if your Ethernet card just isn't running fast enough (if there are a lot of errors or dropped packets).

Route

Since Linux supports multiple interfaces for networking, there has to be a way to determine where packets are supposed to go for each interface. The route program tells the kernel this.

Going back to the loopback device, the route command above tells the kernel that any packets for the 127.0.0.0 network goes through the loopback device. Running route without any options tells us how it's set up:

```
> /sbin/route
Kernel routing table
Destination    Gateway      Genmask        Flags   Metric    Ref      Use Iface
127.0.0.0      *            255.0.0.0      U       0         0        143 lo >
```

The first thing you have to do is add the network and the netmask:

```
# /sbin/route -net 192.5.10.0 netmask 192.5.10.0
```

For a machine that has one Ethernet card, or a stand alone machine that uses PPP or SLIP, the route program will just be used to tell the kernel that the default route is the Ethernet card or the PPP/SLIP device.

```
# /sbin/route add default gw 192.5.10.20
```

Once the command line comes back, the setup is complete and you should be able to connect to another machine on the network.

Dialup

The other way to connect to the Internet is through the use of a dialup protocol. There are two major ones available: SLIP (Serial Line Internet Protocol) and PPP (Point-to-Point Protocol). In many respects, the two are similar: both provide a way to use your serial port (or modem) to connect to another machine and become an Internet host—to send TCP/IP data packets over that serial line.

There are a few differences between the two when you look into how the protocols work.

PPP Advantages:
Built-in compression
More error checking
Can handle protocols other than TCP/IP
Easier to set-up

PPP Disadvantages:
New (in comparison to SLIP), so not as many providers will carry it

SLIP Advantages:
Used longer than PPP
Compression is available through CSLIP (Compressed SLIP)

SLIP Disadvantages:
CSLIP and SLIP are not compatible—both ends must use the same protocol
Not as much error checking as PPP
Can handle only TCP/IP data

The preference is PPP, but since not all Internet service providers provide PPP access, you can use SLIP or CSLIP for access.

PPP/SLIP Setups

The PPP and SLIP packages come with scripts to allow you to easily start and stop connections. There are also some scripts that will automatically start a PPP connection as soon as you try to make a TCP/IP connection. In order to use the PPP connection, you'll need the pppd (or ppp daemon) software installed. The PPP program will install itself in the /usr/lib/ppp directory (or thereabouts). Since this software changes frequently, it is hard to give an actual setup procedure that will work in all situations. If you follow the instructions that come with the software, and know all the network information described above, it should be easy for you to get a connection working. See Appendix B to look at some of the relevant (and more timely) HOWTO files to get some dialup connections working.

CHAPTER
16

- Window Manager

- User Programs

- X Resources

- X Applications

- Compiling X Applications

The X-Window System

Much like Microsoft Windows allows you to have a Graphical User Interface (GUI) to access programs, UNIX's main GUI is the X System. The X-Windowing System is developed by the X Consortium to provide a common window system for just about any operating system. The reason for this is that X is really a protocol, just like TCP/IP is. An advantage to this is that a window for an application that is running on a DEC Alpha machine can be displayed on a PC running Linux, and vice versa.

The X system that Linux uses is called XFree86. It was developed by a team that gets code from the X Consortium. The XFree86 team then modifies the code so that it works with PC hardware, such as the video cards, mice, and so on.

The end result is that you get an implementation of the X-Window System that works with your particular hardware. Most popular ISA, VESA Local Bus (or VLB), and PCI cards work with XFree86. In fact, just about all video cards that support VGA or EGA graphics will run XFree86. Some cards such as those based on the S3, Mach32, or Mach64 accelerated chipsets also work, and you can get graphics very comparable to those you would expect from MS Windows.

The configuration file for XFree86 is called `XF86config`. It can be located in any number of places including `/etc`, `/usr/X11/lib/X11`, or even `/`. Check the XFree86 documentation for the location. This file contains setup information for your mouse, the video card you're using, and the type of display (monitor) that you're using.

The programming for XFree86 allows you, as the user, to set up your monitor and your video card to much better resolutions than you can get by default through Windows or other VGA modes. The default modes (640X480, 800X600, and 1024X768) are still available, and relatively easy to set up. To get custom modes, you'll need some information about the video card (the type of card it is and dot clocks), and some information about your monitor (video bandwidth, horizontal frequency, and vertical frequency). Then you'll need to check the XFree86 documentation about how to put it all together.

To setup your X System configuration with default modes, make sure your X server is installed. For normal VGA modes, this is the x_VGA file. Going from there, the Mach32 server is called XF86_Mach32. When you did your installation, you may have been asked for the type of video card you had. In this case, you can select the server for your particular video card. You may also want to include the regular VGA file just in case.

The XF86config program will allow you to set up some default video modes. Starting the program as root gives a few configuration screens and some text to read. Then you get into the configuration section. Select your mouse type (Microsoft, MouseSystems, Bus). The preference here is to select a three button mouse, since X will allow you to use all three buttons. If you select a two button mouse, you'll need to hit both the left and right mouse buttons to simulate the middle button.

The next few options depend on the type of mouse you selected. If you selected a three button mouse, then you won't need to select Emulate3Buttons. Next you'll need to enter the location of the mouse, which may be /dev/mouse, or could be /dev/ttyS2.

A few other options may follow, including using the ALT key as the "Meta" key to generate characters not normally available on your keyboard.

Next is the monitor configuration section. This is where you need to know the horizontal sync range. There are nine predefined monitors you can choose from, and a tenth allows you to define your own range.

WARNING: Be sure that the numbers entered here are correct because a wrong monitor and video card pair can damage your monitor, video card, or both.

Next is the vertical sync. Here you have a choice of about four monitor types, plus one to let you define your own. Once the vertical sync is set, you can enter information about your monitor. This section isn't necessary, as this allows XFree86 to use multiple monitors at the same time. You can either press enter and use the default for each, or enter in a unique identifier for your monitor, along with a vendor name, and model name.

Once this is completed, you set up the video card. It's important to select the correct video card because two video cards from the same vendor can have very different hardware internally. Selecting the wrong card can damage your card or monitor.

Now you get to select the type of server to run. If you selected a video card that has an accelerator chip supported by XFree86, you'll be able to select that X server. The options are listed here:

1. The XF86_Mono server, which is a 640x480 resolution with two colors, black and white. This should work for all VGA cards. If you suspect a problem with your video card, or are unsure of the type of video card you have, this may be a good starting point.

2. XF86_VGA16 server, which is also 640x480, but at 16 colors. This should also work with all VGA-compatable cards.

3. XF86_SVGA server, which provides SVGA resolutions with 256 colors. This is an unaccelerated server, so most ISA SVGA cards will probably work with it.

4. Accelerated server, which is for accelerated cards. This gives greater than 256 colors for most servers, and higher resolutions. These servers also utilize any of the faster chipsets in most modern video cards.

5. The server for the video card you selected earlier.

If you select 5, the best server for your card is set up for installation.

Now you must give information about your video card. First you'll probably be asked about the amount of video memory on your card. You'll get five selections from 256k to 4096k (4 MB) and a sixth selection that allows you to enter your own amount.

Once that is completed, you'll be allowed to enter in a description for your video card similar to the monitor descriptions above. You can either press enter through the entries, or type in the description, vendor, and model of your video card.

If you have an S3 or AGX based video card, you'll need to know the type of RAMDAC the card has. The RAMDAC is used to get high color (greater than about 32k colors) from the server. Enter in the appropriate entry if you have those cards and know the RAMDAC type, or else you can just press enter.

Some video cards also have a programmable clock. Most clocks are not programmable, but if yours is (some Diamond cards and some S3 cards do), enter the type of clockchip you have. It should be found in your owners manual, or on the card itself. If you don't have a clockchip, just press enter.

At this point, the XF86config program will attempt to find the clocks that your card supports by using the X -probeonly command. This command doesn't start X itself, but asks the video card to return what clocks it knows about. These clocks are important to determine the correct resolutions you can use.

Now you should be ready to start X. Doing this is simply getting to a command prompt and typing:

```
> startx
```

For the sake of extra memory, you may want to log out of other Virtual Consoles before starting X, since you can start multiple shells known as Xterms. You can switch to a virtual console while in X by pressing CTRL-ALT-Fn where n is a number between 1 and 6. The first X server usually uses virtual console 7. You can see what VC is being used when X starts up, or by going through the virtual consoles.

Once you enter the `startx` command, you should see some text fly off the screen. The screen will change to a graphic screen and a mouse cursor. The look here can change based on a few things.

Window Manager

The way that X looks is determined by two things: the type of windows and the window manager. The windows merely interact with the X server and there is no real way of moving the windows around the screen, or resizing the windows. This is where the window manager comes in. The window manager places a border around the window, and can provide maximize (full-screen) or minimize (iconize) buttons. The window manager also allows you to resize, move, or even kill windows.

There are a few different window managers available, such as twm, fvwm, openwin, and the commercially available mwm. Each window manager has its own look, and mwm even has its own header files and libraries to use some extra functions not present in the other window managers. The Openlook Window Manager also has its own extra libraries and interface. The two remaining window managers, twm and fvwm have their specific window borders and default menu options.

Even though the windows look different, they perform many of the same functions. One advantage that fvwm has over twm is that fvwm provides for virtual desktops. That is, you can have more than one main window (also called the root window) available to you at one time. This lets you have a neater X desktop, or it can let you open more windows and be able to see all of them.

User Programs

The default X setup has a bunch of user programs, including shells, utilities, and a couple of games. These programs all have a few default options that you can set when you first start them. I'll show this by introducing the xterm, which is the X terminal emulator. This is almost the same as logging into the shell. The big difference here is that the `.login` file is not read, rather the `.cshrc`.

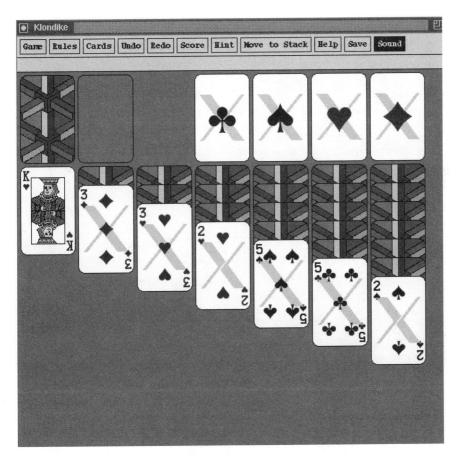

The TWM Window Manager

Here are a few of the common options you can use with almost all X programs:

`-display <host>:<display>`

Sends the display (not just the output) to the named host and display number. In most cases, the display can be 0.0 which means the first X server and the first display on that X server. The program still gets executed on the remote CPU, but the window gets displayed elsewhere. This setting will override the DISPLAY environment variable if it's set. If the DISPLAY variable is set and the -display option is not used, the window will automatically be displayed on the host and display set in DISPLAY.

`-bg <color>`

Sets the color of the background of the window. Color can either be a name of a color ("grey" or "blue") or as collections of RGB values in hex. The syntax for this

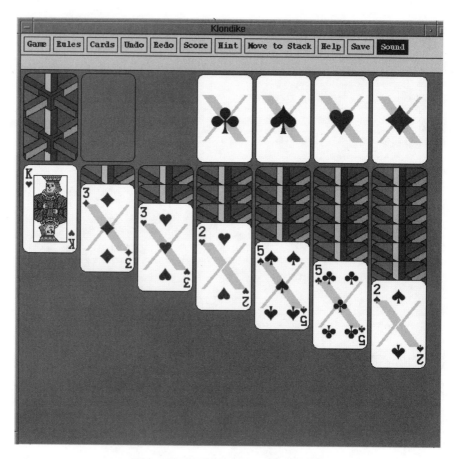

The FVWM Window Manager

is rgb:h/h/h where h is a hex number relating to the amount of red (in the first slot), green (second slot), and blue (third slot) to make a particular color. The hex number can be one to four characters, depending on the number of colors your X server supports. For example, rgb:0/0/0 is black, while rgb:ffff/0/0 is red. A list of colors that have names is available in the /usrX11/lib/X11/rgb.txt file. Each entry has the RGB values in decimal (0 to 255) and a name, which can be used instead of the rgb:h/h/h entry.

-fg <color>

Sets the color of the foreground.

-fn <font>

Specifies the default font to use in the window. You can get lists of the available fonts using the xfontsel or xlsfonts programs.

```
-geometry <WIDTH>x<HEIGHT>+<XOFF>+<YOFF>
```

Sets the size and position of the window. For xterm, this is in terms of characters, so a geometry of

```
> xterm -geometry 80x25
```

would create a window that is 80 characters wide and 25 lines long. The XOFF and YOFF set where the upper left-hand corner of the window should be placed. In the case of positive XOFF or YOFF, the offset is from the left or top sides respectively. For negative XOFF or YOFF, the offset is from the right or bottom sides respectively. Here's some example screen placements:

```
+0+0      Upper left hand corner
-0+0      Upper right hand corner
-0-0      Lower right hand corner
+0-0      Lower left hand corner
```

Note that you can enter either a geometry or an offset, but you can't enter only XOFF or width by itself. The geometry and the offset have to be entered as a pair. That is, you can't enter

```
> xterm -geometry 80
```

or

```
> xterm -geometry +0
```

but the following will work:

```
> xterm -geometry 80x25
```

or

```
> xterm -geometry +0+0
```

There's one other way to specify default settings for X programs, and this is through the .Xdefaults file. Anything you can set through the command line can be stored in the .Xdefaults file so when you start the program, you don't need to give all the options. These options are known as resources.

X Resources

An X resource consists of four items:

```
program.widget[.widget..].resource: value
```

where

program:	Program name
widget:	One or more levels of widgets, which are subportions of the window. A widget can be a button, menu, scrollbar, or option list
resource:	The most specific of the widget list
value:	What the resource gets set to. Can be a number, boolean (true or false), color, or some other value. It depends on the resource.

Any text from a ! to the end of the line is commented out.

The connections between items can be either a period or a star. A period indicates a tight binding and a star represents a loose binding. You don't really need to have all four of the items to make an X resource. Only the resource and the value are needed.

In a loose binding, the link between two widgets does not have to be direct. That is, you can have an entry such as

```
*geometry: 80x25
```

which would say that all geometry settings would be 80x25. While this is good for text-based programs, a graphical application with a setting of 80x25 pixels would be rather small indeed. If you have a specific program, you can then become more specific. That is, if you want all programs that use the vt100 widget to have a geometry of 80x25, you can make the setting like this:

```
*vt100.geometry: 80x25
```

You can get even more specific. Say that you want your terminal emulators to have a size of 80x25, and you want your Seyon(*) emulator to have a size of 80x40. Then you would have two settings of:

```
xterm.vt100.geometry: 80x25
Seyon.vt100.geometry: 80x40
```

Here you have tight bindings. The Seyon program uses the vt100 widget, which then sets the geometry. Using a loose binding for seyon like this:

```
Seyon*geometry: 80x40
```

would cause all of the windows that Seyon creates to be 80x40. Since Seyon creates a few graphical based windows, this would bring us back to having graphical windows that are 80 pixels by 40 pixels.

Note that you can replace tight bindings with loose bindings. The following two entries are identical:

```
Seyon.vt100.geometry: 80x40
Seyon*vt100*geometry: 80x40
```

Here are a few sample entries that apply to the xterm:

```
xterm*scrollBar: true      ! Turn on the scroll bar on the left side
xterm*geometry: 80x25      ! Set the size to 80x25
xterm*background: gray68   ! Gray background
xterm*foreground: black    ! Black characters
```

X Applications

Along with the Xterm emulator, there are a number of other client programs that you can run. All of these are installed as part of a complete X installation. All of the programs also use the -display, -geometry, and -background plus some extra options. Note that while these options override the settings in the .Xdefaults file, it is really up to the Window Manager to make the settings. These options (and the settings in .Xdefaults) are really suggestions to the Window Manager. The Window Manager often allows the requests, but there may be a case where the Window Manager does its own thing.

Here's some of the common X options:

-fg <color> or -foreground <color>	—Foreground color
-fn <font> or -font <font>	—Default font
-iconic	—Start the program as an icon
-title <text>	—Give a window a title

Available X applications:

xmh —E-mail handler
bitmap—Bitmap editor
xman —X interface to the man program
xclock —Digital or analog clock
xcalc —Calculator
xkill —Kill a window
xwd —Dump a window image to a file

There are also other X applications not part of the X project that are installed with Linux:

xv —Image viewer and converter
mosaic —WWW browser
seyon —Communication program
xsysinfo —System information (CPU idle, memory free, and so on)
xpaint —Paint program
xghostview—View PostScript files

Compiling X Applications

Compiling X applications is slightly different than building a regular text-based file. Shared libraries can be in different locations, header file locations, use of motif, and so on. To make the configuration a bit easier, a file called Imakefile is included with most X applications. The Imakefile is sent through a processor (xmkmf which calls a program called imake). The xmkmf program converts the Imakefile to a Makefile. Once this is completed, you can type make to have the program begin compiling.

APPENDIX

A

- USENET

- WWW Resources

- FTP

- E-Mail

- Printed Magazine

Additional Linux Resources

There is a lot of information out on the Internet about setting up Linux and using it. The three biggest locations are USENET (a news facility), WWW, and FTP. While most of these sources of information require an Internet account, there are some resources that do not.

USENET

The following newsgroups have a rather large readership (I see about 100–200 messages per day in most of them). If you post a question to one of these groups, please be sure the question is appropriate to the group.

comp.os.linux.advocacy—Mostly related to Linux in the trade press, and "Linux vs. other operating systems" discussions.

comp.os.linux.announce—Official release information for software related to the Linux system or the kernel.

comp.os.linux.answers—Contains FAQs (Frequently Asked Questions) and HOWTOs.

comp.os.linux.development.system—For discussions related to the kernel.

comp.os.linux.developemnt.apps—For discussions related to applications.

comp.os.linux.hardware—For discussions about hardware compatability and use under Linux.

comp.os.linux.misc—For discussions that don't fit in most other newsgroups.

comp.os.linux.networking—For most forms of Linux netowrking; PPP, Ethernet, ISDN, and so on.

comp.os.linux.x—For setup and install of XFree86.

WWW Resources

There are a number of starting points, and the best way to find most of them is by using a WWW searching site like yahoo (http://www.yahoo.com/) or Lycos (http://www.lycos.com/). Searching for a word like "Linux" will give you a large number of sites, but you can narrow your search by giving more search words. If you want information on PPP, search for "Linux PPP."

Among the more interesting Linux sites that I frequently look at are as follows:

http://www.linux.org or

http://www.ssc.com/linux/linux.html—A good starting point for Linux information. Contains links to FTP sites, manual pages, FAQs, and a link to a program that can find software for you. While the two links are identical, the second one is preferred since http://www.linux.org has a very slow link to the Internet.

http://sunsite.unc.edu/mdw/HOWTO—List of the Linux HOWTO lists, broken down into almost fifty different topics. These HOWTOs have a lot of information in them and cover topics from setting up an Ethernet network to hardware compatability to lists of commercial applications.

http://www.crynwr.com/kchanges/—Contains a list of kernels and the changes that appeared in the kernel since the last version. This is a good way of deciding whether or not you should upgrade to a newer kernel.

http://www.redhat.com/—Contains information about the RedHat distribution, one of the many that exist. Also contains Linux information.

http://www.cdrom.com/—Contains information about the Slackware distribution.

FTP

FTP, or file transfer protocol, is the main way of sending files through the Internet.

nic.funet.fi—The closest thing you can get to an official Linux site. It's located in Finland, so the connections may not be fast or reliable from the U.S.

tsx-11.mit.edu—Located in Boston, MA and is one of the two most-known U.S. sites for Linux programs and information.

sunsite.unc.edu—Located at the University of North Carolina, and is another one of the most popular in the U.S. It has dozens of mirror sites all over the world. These mirror sites allow you to connect to a site closer to you, but get the information from sunsite.

Most CD-ROM disributions of Linux carry copies of the sunsite and tsx-11 FTP sites. This is very helpful if you have a slow link to the Internet or no link at all. You can find links to CD-ROM distributors in the WWW section, or at local computer shows.

E-Mail

There are a few mailing lists that exist for information. Most of them are related to alpha software that may not be ready for a general release. If you're a programmer, the discussions on some of these groups may interest you.

Sending e-mail to majordomo@vger.rutgers.edu with a message of "send index" will send you a list of the mailing lists that you can subscribe to. A message of "send help" will send you instructions on subscribing and unsubscribing to lists.

From here, you will receive messages via e-mail, which you can store and read at a later time if you wish.

Printed Magazine

The Linux Journal is a monthly magazine published since early 1994. It covers a variety of topics from reviews of software and books to system administration articles, programming, beginners columns, and even stories of Linux being used for real-world setups.

You can get more information about *The Linux Journal* with these addresses:

e-mail: subs@ssc.com

WWW: http://www.ssc.com/

phone: 206–782–7733

APPENDIX
B

- Databases

- Data Visualization, CAD

- Development Tools

- Financial Software

- Mathematics

- Network Management

- Text Processing

- X Related Stuff

- Other Software

Commercial
Linux
Packages

Thishis is a partial list of the Commercial HOWTO list. It contains a listing of commercial applications that you can buy to use with Linux. While this list is by no means complete, it is a good indication that commercial companies are developing software for Linux. This list is available along with other HOW-TOs at the following World Wide Web address:

```
http://sunsite.unc.edu/mdw/HOWTO
```

The Commercial HOWTO is covered by the following copyright:

This HOWTO is Copyright (c) 1995 by Harald Milz. Unauthorized reproduction in whatever form is explicitly allowed and strongly encouraged :-) . If you quote the document as a whole or parts of it, you are urged to add a Copyright hint to the derived work.

Databases
AccountFlex

Description:

AccountFlex is a powerful full-featured accounting system that includes modules for Order Entry, Inventory, Purchasing, A/R, A/P, G/L, Payroll, and Jobcost. Accountflex uses Infoflex, an SQL based 4GL lanquage that is compatible with Informix (see information in this HOWTO. hm).

Vendor:

Infoflex Inc.
840 Hinckley Road, Suite 107
Burlingame, CA 94010, USA
Phone: +1 (415) 697–6045
Fax: +1 (415) 697–7696
Contact: Gerard Menicucci

CONZEPT 16

Description:

CONZEPT 16 is a complete software development system based on a relational database. It runs on different platforms and in heterogeneous networks. A version with graphical user interface is available too. Client/server technology is optional. CONZEPT 16 is a high performance system, for which there are hardly limitations.

Vendor:

vectorsoft Gesellschaft fuer Datentechnik mbH
Seligenstaedter Grund 2
D-63150 Heusenstamm, Germany
Phone: +49 6104/6477
Fax: +49 6104/65250
Mailbox: +49 6104/5022

D-ISAM

Description:

Multikey B+ tree Isam File Handler. Follows the C-ISAM (Informix) file structure and function calls. Sold with Source.

Vendor:

Byte Designs Ltd
20568 - 32 Avenue
Langley, BC V3A 4P5, Canada
Phone: +1 (604) 534–0722
Fax: +1 (604) 534–2601
E-mail: sales@byted.com
Contact: Heinz Wittenbecher

Empress RDBMS

Description:

The port to Linux provides customers a choice of two levels of product: A) full function RDBMS B) single user Personal EMPRESS for Linux. A) EMPRESS RDBMS is a powerful application development tool which provides heterogeneous distributed processing capabilities. Its features include data manipulation options, integrity and recovery features, portability, and unlimited storage capacity. B) Personal EMPRESS for Linux is a low-cost, single-user version designed especially for the rapidly growing Linux users community. It includes Version 6.6 of the EMPRESS RDBMS and 4GL application generator; SQL, Dynamic SQL and host language C interface; and the EMPRESS GUI Builder for Motif. This product is available via catalog through the ACC Bookstore.

Vendor:

A) Empress Software Inc.
6401 Golden Triangle Drive
Greenbelt, MD 20770, USA
Phone: +1 (301) 220–1919
Fax: +1 (301) 220–1997
E-mail: sales@empress.com
Contact: Jim Sweeney

B) ACC Bookstore
Phone: +1 (800) 546–7274
E-mail: bob@redhat.com
Contact: Bob Young

ESQLFlex

Description:

ESQLFlex is a low-cost clone of the Informix-ESQL/C and Informix standard Engine products. ESQLFlex will allow developers to completely replace Informix-ESQL and Informix standard engine without having to modify their existing application. ESQLFlex enables developers to build, modify, and/or query databases using standard SQL calls from within C programs.

Vendor:

Infoflex Inc.
840 Hinckley Road, Suite 107
Burlingame, CA 94010, USA
Phone: +1 (415) 697–6045
Fax: +1 (415) 697–7696
Contact: Gerard Menicucci

InfoFlex

Description:

InfoFlex is a complete 4GL that streamlines the design process with a consistent WYSIWYG approach to developing menus, screens, and reports. Infoflex is compatible with the Informix database and is similar in syntax. Demos, source, and unlimited licenses are available for UNIX, DOS, or VMS.

Vendor:

Infoflex Inc.
840 Hinckley Road, Suite 107
Burlingame, CA 94010, USA
Phone: +1 (415) 697–6045
Fax: +1 (415) 697–7696
Contact: Gerard Menicucci

Just Logic/SQL Database Manager

Description:

The Just Logic/SQL Database Manager is a relational database system made to
be used from C and C++ applications. It includes a complete set of libraries, utilities, and a database engine. It comes with three programming interfaces: a C API
interface, a C++ Class definitions, and a C Precompiler. The client/server version
permits Windows and Unix applications to access a remote server on Unix across
TCP/IP. WWW: http://www.pht.com/justlogic/

Vendor:

Just Logic Technologies Inc.
P.O. Box 63050
40 Commerce St.
Nun's Island, Quebec H3E 1V6, Canada
Phone: +1 (800) 267–6887 (toll free USA and Canada)
        +1 (514) 761–6887
Fax: +1 (514) 642–6480 (has voice-fax autodetection)
E-mail: 71563.3370@CompuServe.COM

POET 2.1

Description:

POET 2.1 ODBMS for C++ has database functionality for C++ objects. Full support of encapsulation, inheritance, polymorphism, and object identity. Two versions are available: Personal Edition (Single/User 1 Developer), Professional Edition (Client/Server up to 4 Developers).

Vendor:

POET Software GmbH
Fossredder 12
D-22359 Hamburg, Germany
Phone: +49 (0)40/609 90 18
Fax: +49 (0)40/603 98 51
E-mail: info@poet.de
Contact: Detlef Meyer

/rdb

Description:

/rdb is a RDBMS consisting of more than 125 shell level commands which read tables from the standard input and write tables to the standard output. Applications are typically written in shell scripts, mixing /rdb commands with ordinary system commands. A runtime library is also included.

Revolutionary Software
131 Rathburn Way
Santa Cruz, CA 95062–1035
Phone: +1 (408) 429 6229
E-mail: rdb@rsw.com
Contact: Evan Schaffer

Veritas

Description:

Veritas is a system for German drink wholesalers ("Getrönkegrosshöndler"). It's based on Onyx which is my 4GL and database project, which of course stays under the GNU Public License 2.0 . Ftp to wowbagger.pc-labor.uni-bremen.de if you like to take a look at Onyx.

The first version of Veritas was developed for PCOS Olivetti in 1992, later Xenix versions followed. The recent third release features twelve years of experience with this kind of market, so you can expect to have nearly anything a drink wholesaler needs; and so on. Pfand, Sektsteuer, Brauereiabrechung, Bruchvergütung, and so on.

Several servers can be linked via SLIP or UUCP and replicate transactions to share data. Clients are connected via Ethernet to a local server and can run MS Windows or Linux.

Vendor:

Michael Koehne
Loss Datensysteme
Bremerstr. 117
D-28816 Brinkum, Germany
Phone: +49 (0)421/87 55 00
V32bis: +49 (0)421/87 05 32
Fax: +49 (0)421/87 55 51
E-mail: kraehe@nordwest.de (company)
        kraehe@bakunin.north.de (private)

Yard SQL

Description:

The YARD company offers five SQL products as follows:

YARD-SQL—Relational SQL database server with compliance to X/Open XPG4 and ANSI SQL 92

YARD-ESQLC—Embedded SQL for C

YARD-ODBC—ODBC interface for MS Windows clients

YARD-NET — Remote access to YARD databases via TCP/IP

YARD-X—Motif client for database access (no development tool).

Vendor:

YARD Software GmbH
Hansestr. 99
D-51149 Koeln, Germany
Phone: +49 (0)22 03/45 71 30
Fax: +49 (0)22 03/45 71 31
E-mail: yard@yard.de
Contact: Thomas Schonhoven (thomass@yard.de)

Data Visualization, CAD

CAD tools, renderers, OCR software and such stuff.

Ghostscript 3.x

Description:

Aladdin Ghostscript 3.n is a full PostScript Level 2 language interpreter. It can display PostScript files on the screen with X-Windows, convert them to various raster formats (TIFF/F, GIF, PCX, PPM), and print them on many non-PostScript printers, such as the H-P inkjet and laser printers.

Vendor:

Aladdin Enterprises
203 Santa Margarita Ave.
Menlo Park, CA 94025, USA
Phone: +1 (415) 322–0103
Fax: +1 (415) 322–1734
E-mail: ghost@aladdin.com

IDL

Description:

IDL is the pioneering software for data analysis, visualization, and application development. IDL's features include flexible I/O, 2D plotting, 3D graphics, volume rendering, image processing, mathematics, statistics, a cross-platform GUI toolkit, plus a high-level, array-oriented programming language. Use IDL for visual data analysis, rapid prototyping, or application development. IDL programs are portable across Linux, Windows 3.1, Windows 95, Windows NT, Mac, PowerMac, UNIX, and VMS.

Vendor:

Research Systems, Inc.
2995 Wilderness Place
Boulder, Colorado, USA
Phone: +1 (303) 786–9900
Fax: +1 (303) 786–9909
E-mail: info@rsinc.com

Distributor for Central Europe:

CREASO GmbH
Phone: +49 81 05/250 55
E-mail: 100137.2421@compuserve.com

MRJ Symbolic OCR

Description:

MRJ SOCR (Symbolic OCR) (TM) is an OCR program for Japanese text. SOCR reads TIFF files and recognizes Japanese text in scanned images. Output formats include PC, Mac, and Unix formats with Unicode, Shift-JIS, JIS, and EUC encodings. Also available for Sun OS.

Vendor:

MRJ, Inc.
10455 White Granite Drive
Oakton, VA 22124, USA
Phone: +1 (703) 385–0700
Fax: +1 (703) 385–4637
E-mail: socr@mrj.com

SISCAD-P 1.3–3

Description:

SISCAD-P is a 2D-CAD system that gives engineers a production implementation of new design technologies—parametrics, variational geometry, inference sketching, a fully customizable user interface, constraint-based modeling, and feature-based modeling. Today there is only a German version of SISCAD-P available. Unfortunately we cannot yet provide a SISCAD-P version in any foreign language but we are already working on an English version. The release date for this version is not certain yet.

Vendor:

Staedtler Mars GmbH & Co
Geschaeftsbereich Informationssysteme—SIS
Moosaeckerstrasse 3
D-90427 Nuernberg, Germany
Phone: +49 (0)911/3080–691
Fax: +49 (0)911/3080–692
BBS: +49 (0)911/3080–609, login: info, password: gast
E-mail: support@SIS.Staedtler.DE
Contact: Helmrich Streitmatter

TecPlot 6.0

Description:

Tecplot is a plotting program for visualizing and analyzing engineering and scientific data. The standard version includes XY, 2D, and 3D-surface plotting. An optional extension (called 3DV) adds the capability to visualize 3D volumetric data. With Tecplot you don't have to write a program, just input your data and start visualizing immediately (for more information consult vendor. hm).

Vendor:

Amtec Engineering, Inc
PO Box 3633
Bellevue, WA 98009–3633, USA
Phone: +1 (206) 827–3304 (800–676–7568 in US/Canada)
Fax: +1 (206) 827–3989
E-mail: tecplot@amtec.com
Contact: Tom Chan

For Germany:

GENIAS Software GmbH
Erzgebirgstr. 2
D-93073 Neutraubling, Germany
Phone: +49 (0)94 01/92 00–11
Fax: +49 (0)94 01/92 00–92
E-mail: jo@genias.de
Contact: Johannes Grawe

Development Tools

Compilers, development environments, and so on.

Basmark QuickBASIC

Description:

The Basmark QuickBASIC Compiler is a multi-user IBM-PC BASICA, MBASIC, and Microsoft QuickBASIC Compiler designed to provide performance and consistency across a variety of machines (e.g. i386 and i486, Pentium, SPARC, RS/6000, HP PA-Risc) under Unix, AIX, SunOS, Linux, HP-UX, and Xenix.

Vendor:

Basmark Corporation
P.O. Box 40450
Cleveland, OH 44140, USA
Phone: +1 (216) 871–8855
Fax: +1 (216) 871–9011
E-mail: jgo@ios.com (for orders)
Contact: Joseph O'Toole (for orders)

CODINE

Description:

CODINE Job Management System—A job-queueing system that allows optimal utilization of a heterogeneous workstation cluster. The system features static and dynamic loadbalancing, checkpointing, support for parallel programs, and so on. It is available for SUN, HP, IBM, SGI, CRAY, CONVEC, DEC, and LINUX

Vendor:

GENIAS Software GmbH
Erzgebirgstr. 2
D-93073 Neutraubling, Germany
Tel.: 09401/9200–11,
Fax: 09401/9200–92
Phone: +49 94 01/92 00–11
Fax: +49 94 01/92 00–92
E-mail: jo@genias.de
Contact: Johannes Grawe

Distributed Interface Object Server System (DIOSS)

Description:

DIOSS is a high-level C Language API to an RPC based daemon that provides Motif 2.0 interfaces. It includes an Interface Builder Tool (DiossLive) and a Distributed Database Daemon. All daemons are freely distributed.

Vendor:

DIOSS Corp.
5205 Leesburg pike—Suite 1200
Phone: +1 (703) 671–0706
Fax: +1(703) 671–5734
E-mail: toneil@in-tech.com
Contact: Tom ONeil

Dynace

Description:

Dynace (pronounced like dynasty without the t) is a preprocessor that includes files and a library which extends the C language with advanced object-oriented capabilities, automatic garbage collection, and multiple threads. Dynace is designed to solve many of the problems associated with C++. It is easier to learn and contains more flexible object-oriented facilities. Dynace is able to add facilities previously only available in languages such as Smalltalk and CLOS without all the overhead normally associated with those environments.

Vendor:

Algorithms Corporation
3020 Liberty Hills Drive
Franklin, TN 37064, USA
Phone: +1 (800) 566–8991 or +1 (615) 791–1636
Fax: +1 (516) 791–7736
E-mail: blake@edge.net
Contact: Blake McBride

Finesse

Description:

OSF/Motif GUI for shell scripts.

Vendor:

science + computing GmbH
Hagellocher Weg 71
D-72070 Tuebingen, Germany
Phone: +49 (0) 7071/9457–0
Fax: +49 (0) 7071/9457–27
E-mail: info@science-computing.uni-tuebingen.de
WWW: http://www.science-computing.uni-tuebingen.de/
Contact: Olaf Flebbe

Flagship

Description:

CA-Clipper5, Fox, dBase, and beyond for Unix. XBase 4GL applications development system and database. Superset of CA-Clipper. Can be used to port.

Vendor:

multisoft Datentechnik GmbH
PO Box 312
D-82027 Gruenwald, Germany
Phone: +49 (0)89/6417904
Fax: +49 (0)89/6412974
E-mail: 100031.267@compuserve.com
Contact: Dorte Balek

North America:

WorkGroup Solutions, Inc
PO Box 460190
Aurora, CO 80046–0190, USA
Phone: +1 (303) 699–7470
Fax: +1 (303) 699–2793
E-mail: info@wgs.com
Contact: Virginia Lane

ICC11

Description:

ICC11 is a full-featured C Compiler for the HC11 microcontrollers: including floating point support, interspersed C and assembly listing, and much more. It's available in native Linux version, as well as DOS and OS2 versions.

Vendor:

ImageCraft
P.O. Box 64226
Sunnyvale, CA 94088–4226, USA
Phone/Fax: +1 (408) 749–0702
E-mail: imagecft@netcom.com
Contact: Richard Man or Christina Willrich

INSURE++

Description:

INSURE++ runtime debugger for C and C++ programms. INSURE detects memory leaks and problems in memory mismanagements during runtime.

Vendor:

GENIAS Software GmbH
Erzgebirgstr. 2
D-93073 Neutraubling, Germany
Tel.: 09401/9200–11, Fax: 09401/9200–92
Phone: +49 94 01/92 00–11
Fax: +49 94 01/92 00–92
E-mail: jo@genias.de
Contact: Johannes Grawe

ISE Eiffel 3

Description:

ISE Eiffel 3 provides a powerful and user-friendly O-O programming environment designed for large, complex systems. It is an integrated GUI workbench consisting of a variety of Eiffel-based components: EiffelBench melting-ice workbench, EiffelBuild interface builder and application generator, EiffelVision graphics and GUI library, and EiffelBase basic libraries.

Vendor:

Interactive Software Engineering, Inc.
270 Storke Road, Suite 7
Goleta, CA 93117, USA
Phone: +1 (805) 685–1006
Fax: +1 (805) 685–6869
E-mail: queries@eiffel.com

Metacard

Description:

MetaCard is a hypermedia/Rapid Application Development environment for X11/Unix workstations that is compatible with Apple Corporation's HyperCard. MetaCard can be used by programmers and sophisticated end-users to build Motif applications and hypermedia documents using a powerful, direct manipulation editor and a simple scripting language. Stacks developed with MetaCard are portable among all supported platforms (14 for release 1.3) and can be distributed with the MetaCard engine without licensing fees or royalties.

Vendor:

MetaCard Corporation
4710 Shoup Pl.
Boulder, CO 80303, USA
Phone: +1 (303) 447–3936
Fax: +1 (303) 499–9855
E-mail: info@metacard.com
Contact: Scott Raney

Mjolner BETA System

Description:

The Mjolner BETA System is a software development environment supporting object-oriented programming in the BETA programming language. BETA is uniquely expressive and orthogonal among object-oriented languages. BETA unifies just about every abstraction mechanism, including class, procedure, function, coroutine, process, and exception, into the ultimate abstraction mechanism: the pattern. In addition it has general block structure, strong typing, whole/part-objects, and concurrency. Compiler: native code generation, garbage collection, separate compilation, C, and assembler interface. System: persistence, distribution, comprehensive libraries, platform-independent GUI application framework (Unix, Mac, Windows, NT), metaprogramming system, graphical system, hyper-structure editor.

Among the unique characteristics of the Mjolner BETA System are that the GUI applications run on Motif, Windows NT, and Macintosh without any change and with the native look and feel; it is easy to write distributed applications and it is easy to save and restore objects from a persistent store.

The Mjolner BETA System is being used successfully for teaching first grade and second grade students at several universities.

Vendor:

Mjolner Informatics Aps
Science Park Aarhus
Gustav Wieds Vej 10
DK-8000 Aarhus C, Denmark
Phone: +45 86 20 20 00
Fax: +45 86 20 12 22
E-mail: info@mjolner.dk, usergroup-request@mjolner.dk, sales@mjolner.dk
Contact: Peter Andersen (Peter.Andersen@mjolner.dk)

SEDIT, S/REXX

Description:

SEDIT is a powerful UNIX (tm) text editor patterned after IBM's XEDIT editor. It operates with a GUI under X-Windows or in character mode from a tty device. S/REXX is a full UNIX implementation of IBM's SAA procedural language except that the numeric digit specification is limited to fifteen digits. S/REXX functions as an imbedded macro langauge for SEDIT as well as providing a powerful modern programming language alternative to shell scripting languages. SEDIT and S/REXX may be purchased in a bundle or individually. See http://www.portal.com/~sedit or http://www.sedit.com/sedit for more information including introductory pricing for Linux. The ftp directory includes a .txt file flattened from the above web pages for users without WWW capability or e-mail.

Vendor:

Benaroya
31 Rue de Constantinople
F-75008 Paris, France
Phone: +33 1 47 22 22 13
Fax: +33 1 47 22 06 17
E-mail: sedit@shell.portal.com
Contact: Robert Benaroya

tgdb

Description:

tgdb is a graphical user interface for gdb, the GNU debugger.

Vendor:

HighTec EDV-Systeme GmbH
Neue Bahnhofstr. 37
D-66386 St. Ingbert, Germany
Phone: +49 (0)6894/87 00 41
Fax: +49 (0)6894/87 00 44
E-mail: tgdb@hightec.saarlink.de
Contact: Michael Schumacher

TowerEiffel

Description:
TowerEiffel is a complete software engineering tool for creating scalable systems in the object-oriented programming language Eiffel. TowerEiffel for Linux includes a high performance Eiffel 3 compiler, open development environment, programming tools including debugger, browser, and automatic documentation generation, and a base set of reusable software components. Key features include fast executable code, global system optimization, user controllable garbage collection, clear and precise error messages, exception handling, genericity, automatic system builds, automatic documentation generation, and built-in test support. A unique capability of TowerEiffel is Eiffel, C, and C++ interoperability.

Vendor:

Tower Technology Corporation
1501 West Koenig Lane
Austin, TX 78756, USA
Phone: (800) 285–5124 or +1 (512) 452–9455
Fax: +1 512 452 1721
E-mail: tower@twr.com
www: http://www.cm.cf.ac.uk/Tower/

Financial Software

All about financial tools.

BB Tool

Description:

BB Tool is a powerful stock charting, technical analysis and portfolio management tool.

Vendor:

Falkor Technologies
P.O. Box 14201
Fremont, CA 94539, U.S.A.
Phone: +1 (510) 505–0700
E-mail: ctor@shell.portal.com
Contact: Henry Chen

Mathematics

Mathematics can as well be done with Linux ...

Maple V

Description:

Maple V Release 3 is a powerful general purpose computer algebra system. Maple V is a system for solving mathematical problems symbolically (instead of using paper and pencil and a lot of time) and numerically. Maple V's graphics (various types of 2D, 3D, animation) visualize the solutions. Maple V has also a programming language (Pascal like) which allows the user to extend the library of 2500+ functions.

Vendor:

Waterloo Maple Software
450 Phillip Street
Waterloo, Ontario, Canada N2L 5J2
Phone: +1 (519) 747–2373
Fax: +1 (519) 747–5284
E-mail: info@maplesoft.on.ca

Germany, Switzerland, and Austria:

Scientific Computers GmbH
Franzstr. 106
D-52064 Aachen, Germany
Phone: +49 (0)241/26041
Fax: +49 (0)241/44983
E-mail: info@scientific.de
Contact: Monika Germ

Mathematica

Description:

Mathematica is a computational and visualization software package that's used by engineers and scientists worldwide for quick, accurate numeric and symbolic answers.

Vendor:

Wolfram Research, Inc.
Phone: +1 (800) 441–6284 or +1 (217) 398–0700
E-mail: info@wri.com
WWW: http://www.wri.com

Europe:

Wolfram Research Europe Ltd.
Phone: +44–(0)1993–883400
E-mail: info-euro@wri.com

MATLAB and SIMULINK

Description:

MATLAB is a high-performance, interactive numeric computation and visualization environment that combines the advantages of hundreds of packaged advanced math and graphics functions with a high-level language.

SIMULINK is a powerful, interactive software package for modeling, analyzing, and simulating dynamic nonlinear systems.

Vendor:

The MathWorks, Inc.
24 Prime Park Way
Natick, MA 01760, USA
Phone: +1 (508) 653–1415 x4322
Fax: +1 (508) 653–2997
E-mail: brian@mathworks.com, efroio@mathworks.com
Contact: Technical: Brian Bourgault, Marketing: Enza Froio
WWW: http://www.mathworks.com

REDUCE

Description:

REDUCE is a general purpose system for the symbolic manipulation of mathematical formulae (computer algebra) in science and engineering. Gather more information via WWW.

Vendor:

Konrad-Zuse-Zentrum Berlin
Heilbronner Str. 10
D-10711 Berlin-Wilmersdorf, Germany
Phone: +49 (0)30/89604–195
Fax: +49 (0)30/89604–125
E-mail: melenk@zib-berlin.de
Contact: H. Melenk

Network Management

Network management tools that are Linux based can save quite a bit on your budget.

Galacticomm BBS

Description:

Worldgroup for UNIX, a client/server on-line software platform integrating workgroup/e-mail applications, commercial on-line services, and BBS technology.

Vendor:

Galacticomm, Inc.
4101 SW 47 Avenue, Suite 101
Ft. Lauderdale, FL 33314, USA
Phone: +1 (305) 583–5990, +1 (800) 328–1128
Fax: +1 (305) 583–7846
E-mail: unix@unix.gcomm.com

NetEye

Description:

NetEye is a complete SNMP-based Network Management System. NetEye's main features are as follows:

Standard X-Window System and OSF/Motif user interface

Autodiscovery and automapping of all IP based objects

MIB Browser to simplify the navigation of all MIB-2 and private enterprise variables

Trouble ticketing system capable of storing and forwarding tickets via e-mail and fax

Capture, filtering, and storing of SNMP device traps

Topological, logical, and spatial network views using color codes

User definable bitmaps to represent network objects on maps

User definable alarm and warning thresholds and time plots of any number of MIB variables

Built-in address book to store and retrieve all fax and e-mail addresses of other network managers

Online hyperhelp for unexperienced operators.

Vendor:

Soft*Star s.r.l.
Via Camburzano 9
10143 Torino, Italy
Phone: +39 11 746092
Fax: +39 11 746487
E-mail: softstar@pol88a.polito.it
        eb@relay1.iunet.it
Contact: Enrico Badella

Venus

Description:

Venus is a distributed administration tool for any network built of Unix workstations from different hardware vendors. A VENUS network presents itself to the user as a homogeneous computer system and guarantees transparent access to any network resource. It provides software tools for major cluster management tasks: configuration management, software distribution, user and filesystem administration.

Vendor:

science + computing GmbH
Hagellocher Weg 71
D-72070 Tuebingen, Germany
Phone: +49 (0) 7071/9457–0
Fax: +49 (0) 7071/9457–27
E-mail: info@science-computing.uni-tuebingen.de
WWW: http://www.science-computing.uni-tuebingen.de/
Contact: Olaf Flebbe

VU-BBS

Description:

Visually oriented BBS system and system/user administration package. VU BBS offers tools for installing and managing a large and active site as well as providing an easy to use and yet powerful commercial BBS environment.

Vendor:

Tycho Softworks
25 Ceder St.
Garfield, NJ 07026, USA
E-mail: mycroft@mnsinc.com
Contact: David Sugar

Text Processing

All kind of text processing, ASCII- and GUI-based

CRISP

Description:

CRISP is a graphical text editor based on various Unix and Windows platforms which is 100% compatible with BRIEF. What makes Crisp different is that it tries to deliver its power in an intuitive point and click environment, without taking away the keyboard.

Vendor:

VITAL SOLUTIONS INC
4109 Candlewyck Drive
Plano, TX 75024, USA
Phone: +1 (214) 491–6907
Fax: +1 (214) 491–6909
E-mail: info@vital.com
Contact: Gigi Mehrotra

ibgsXaed

Description:

ibgsXaed is an editor that is portable to every X-Window System that offers OSF/Motif. The editor has normal edit functions and a lot of special features that support newcomers and professionals (f.e. function keys for system commands execution, variable fonts, undo, redo, online help, hotlist, iconbar).

Vendor:

ibgs GmbH
Promenade 7
D-52076 Aachen, Germany
Phone: +49 (0)2408/9455–53
Fax: +49 (0)2408/9455–15
Contact: Mr.Sohn

X Related Stuff

Alternative X servers, widget sets, window managers.

Metrolink Motif

Description:

Motif 1.2.4—Graphical User Interface is a complete runtime and development package with color pixmap support.

Vendor:

Metro Link Incorporated
4711 N. Powerline Rd.
Fort Lauderdale, FL 33309, USA
Phone: +1 (305) 938–0283
Fax: +1 (305) 938–1982
E-mail: sales@metrolink.com (general info)
Contact: Holly Robinson (holly@metrolink.com, other questions & orders)

X Inside X Servers

Description:

Replacement X Server for the XFree86 and other servers for Linux. Supports Actix, ColorGraphics, Compaq, ELSA, Matrox, Number 9, ATI, Boca, Diamond, Orchid, Reveal, STB, TechWorks. Chipsets include Matrox, Number 9 Imagine-128, ATI Mach64, and S3 964. Supports Mouse Systems, Microsoft, and Logitech mice.

Vendor:

X Inside Incorporated
P.O. Box 10774
Golden, CO 80401–0610, USA
Phone: +1 (303) 384–9999
Fax: +1 (303) 384–9778
E-mail: info@xinside.com

Europe:

delix Computer GmbH
Schloss-Str. 98
D-70176 Stuttgart, Germany
Phone: +49 711/621027–0
Fax: +49 711/613590
E-mail: info@delix.de

Other Software

Everything else that does not fit in one of the other sections by now.

Amadeus Music Software

Description:

Fully professional music notation and printing software. Supports MIDI-interface for realtime and step input. Printer drivers to some matrix-, ink-jet, and laserprinters. Supports postscript translation for output on PS-printers or use in Ghostscript for printing on any printer supported by GS. Supports TIFF (import and export). The functionality is somewhat roff or TEX look a like. ASCII-files (one per system) containing source are processed into files, containing one page each, which can be converted into graphic files for viewing or editing on screen or printing, or into other formats as PS or TIFF. The software is highly automated in the actual note drawing. This makes it possible for blind musicians to print music for seeing if they use a blindsign-display to handle the computer.

Vendor:

Wolfgang Hamann
Amadeus Notenzats
Winterstr. 5
D-81543 Muenchen, Germany
Phone: +49 89 669678
Fax: +49 89 669579
Contact: Wolfgang Hamann

Scandinavian customers and e-mail:

Jerker Elsgard
MIDIBIT AB
Box 161
S-618 23 Kolmarden, Sweden
Phone/Fax: +46 11 391663
E-mail: m8770@abc.se
Contact: Jerker Elsgard

aqua_zis

Description:

Time Series Information System—a system to store and maintain huge amounts of measurement data (mainly hydrological data). Time series with several hundreds of thousands of values can be handled. You may retrieve, edit, and insert data very fast. A lot of statistical and arithmetical operators are applicable. Time series may be visualized in a full-scale GUI, including high-performance zooming ans scrolling. The user may define individual GUI's in an easy script language and with the time series programming language Azur. Reports on any paper size including full graphics are possible through Azur. Output is produced in Postscript and HPGL formats.

Vendor:

aqua_plan
Ing.-Ges. fuer Problemloesungen
in Hydrologie und Umweltschutz mbH
Mozartstr. 16
D-52064 Aachen, Germany
Phone: +49 (0)241/31430
Fax: +49 (0)241/31499

CLiX

Description:

CliX is a OSF/Motif based desktop available for almost any UNIX platform, providing support for remote and local files and directory manipulations. It handles print and batch queues and message based communication.

Vendor:

science + computing GmbH
Hagellocher Weg 71
D-72070 Tuebingen, Germany
Phone: +49 (0) 7071/9457–0
Fax: +49 (0) 7071/9457–27
E-mail: info@science-computing.uni-tuebingen.de
WWW: http://www.science-computing.uni-tuebingen.de/
Contact: Olaf Flebbe

Executor

Description:

Commercial Macintosh emulator with fast CPU emulation (75 MHz 486DX4 approximates 25 MHz 68040). Allows many Macintosh applications, including Word 5 and Excel 4 to run without requiring anything from Apple. Reads, writes, and formats 1.4 MB Macintosh formatted floppies. Reads and writes SCSI Macintosh disks. Reads Macintosh formatted CD-ROMs. It has color support and prints to PostScript printers. Has demo applications so you can run it with no Macintosh experience.

Vendor:

ARDI
Suite 4–101
1650 University Blvd., NE
Albuquerque, NM 87102
Phone: +1 (505) 766 9115
Fax: +1 (505) 247 1899
E-mail: questions@ardi.com, orders@ardi.com, bugs@ardi.com

Mazama Packet Filter

Description:

The Mazama Packet Filter is a Linux-based IP packet filtering or firewall application.

Vendor:

Mazama Software Labs, Inc.
15600 NE 8th St., Suite B1 #544
Bellevue, WA 98008
Phone: +1 (206) 545–1808
E-mail: info@mazama.com (general inquiries), support@mazama.com
   (tech support)
Contact: Eric D. Berg

PROCHEM-C

Description:

PROCHEM-C is an integrated software system for users dealing with design, construction, maintenance, operation, and control of plants in the fields of

—Pipeline construction
—Chemical & pharmaceutical industry
—Power plant construction
—Petrochemical industry
—Food processing
—Environment technology.

Vendor:

COMPLANSOFT CAD GmbH
Sulzbacher Strasse 15 - 21
D-65812 Bad Soden, Germany
Phone: +49 6196/56 06–0
Fax : +49 6196/56 06–66
Contact : Chris Chirila

ROSIN NC

Description:

ROSIN-NC-Werkbank (ger: workbench) The ROSIN-NC-Werkbank is a comprehensive set of tools that accomplish a CAD system. These tools comprise the ROSIN-VDAFS-Processor to process digitized data, and data in the VDAFS format; the ROSIN-Post Processors to generate 2- to 5-axis milling programs for all major CNC process controls; the ROSIN-NC-Editor to analyse and edit existing NC programs; the ROSIN-NC-Visualizer to visualize the tool path and generate printed information about a NC program; the ROSIN-Engraver to mill logos or fonts of any kind.

Vendor:

ROSIN Gesellschaft fuer technische Datenverarbeitung mbH
Roniger Weg 13
D-53545 Linz am Rhein, Germany
Phone: +49 (0)2644/97003–0
Fax: +49 (0)2644/97003–32
Contact: Gisela Buechner (Marketing)

SPATCH

Description:

SPATCH software allows alphanumeric paging from a Linux system. With SPATCH, Linux users can send text messages to alphanumeric pagers from a user, an application, an operating system, or an e-mail system.

Vendor:

The Hyde Company, Inc.
P.O. Box 900190
Atlanta, GA 30329, USA
Phone: +1 (770) 495–0718
Fax: N/A
E-mail: spatch@cy.com
Contact: Alan Lewis

Unix Cockpit

Description:

The Unix Cockpit (UC) is a nifty new file manager for Unix/X11 that smoothly integrates a directory tree, file browsers, custom menus, and the classic Unix shells into one highly customizable productivity tool of a kind long-missed on Unix systems.

Vendor:

Henrik Klagges
UniX11 Software Development Corp
Moorbachweg 7
D-83209 Prien, Germany
E-mail: henrik@UniX11.com

Unix Auto-Tutor

Description:

Unix Auto-Tutor is an automatic Unix tutor—a comprehensive, fully interactive, self-teaching CBT system for Unix training. It is organized like a traditional textbook with hypertext pages. Currently it has nine chapters and seventy-six sections with eighty-seven interactive tutorial sessions attached to its hypertext pages. More than 150 Unix commands, such as find, grep, sort, sed, awk, and vi, are introduced. It can be used to provide in-house training or on-line training through BBS or Internet.

Vendor:

Sunny Micro Lab
1300 Britannia Road East, Suite #208
Mississauga, Ontario L4W 1C8, Canada
Phone: +1 (905) 795–9292
Fax: +1 (905) 795–9291
E-mail: info@sunni.com or sunni@hookup.net
Contact: Mo Chen

INDEX